A Guide to Tudor & Jacobean Portraits

Tarnya Cooper
Foreword by Antonia Fraser

National Portrait Gallery
in association with the National Trust

Foreword

Where historical biography is concerned, I have always been an enthusiast for what I call 'optical research': in plain words, going and looking hard at the people I'm going to write about. And then looking again. But a desire to understand the people who shaped our destiny via the painted image is not limited to historians: it can and should overcome anyone with a love of history. The deliberate imposition of an ageless imperial image of Queen Elizabeth I when she was over sixty; the robust masculine sex appeal of her early favourite the Earl of Leicester; the dashing Sir Walter Ralegh with his pearl-encrusted cloak reminding us of the one he is said to have cast so chivalrously before the Queen; the emphasis of the great humanist Sir Thomas More on 'family values' as he stands in a tender domestic group; the love of finery of James I's Queen Anne of Denmark, patroness of the architect Inigo Jones: all these are displayed before our eyes in the National Portrait Gallery's rich panoply and in many country houses throughout Britain. After all, how would we have understood the awe his contemporaries felt for Henry VIII without Hans Holbein the Younger's terrifying yet majestic interpretation? It helps as we gaze to remember that we are not intruders. Most of these pictures were deliberately aimed at us, the public: thus we are seeing kings, queens, princes and notables as they wished to be seen. Looking hard at portraits makes courtiers of us all.

Antonia Fraser

Contents

Introduction

Portraits of people wearing sumptuous fabrics, jewels and impressive wide lace collars illuminate our understanding of the past and provide a focus for our imagination. Portraits tell us about the physical appearance of famous individuals and show us what people wore, but most of all they reveal how people wanted to be remembered. How far a portrait captures the true likeness of a person long since dead is impossible to know. We do know, however, that Tudor and Jacobean artists were meticulous at rendering detail and that patrons often considered portraits as a faithful record of an exact moment in time. On the other hand, individuals also liked portraits to enhance their status and sitters are often shown wearing their best outfits and posed to reveal their most virtuous characteristics.

The rise of portraiture

The type of framed life-sized portraits we know today arrived late in Britain. By the later 1400s portraiture was a feature of life at the courts of European monarchs, yet in England very few portraits were painted before 1500. Prior to this portraits occasionally appeared in manuscript illumination, but it was not until the reign of Henry VIII that life-sized painted portraiture gained popularity and was regularly employed to depict monarchs and other members of the royal court.

In the later sixteenth century portraits became increasingly popular for men and women outside the court circle, including merchants and other wealthy citizens. By 1600 we find writers, composers, lawyers and other aspiring young gentlemen commissioning their own likenesses.

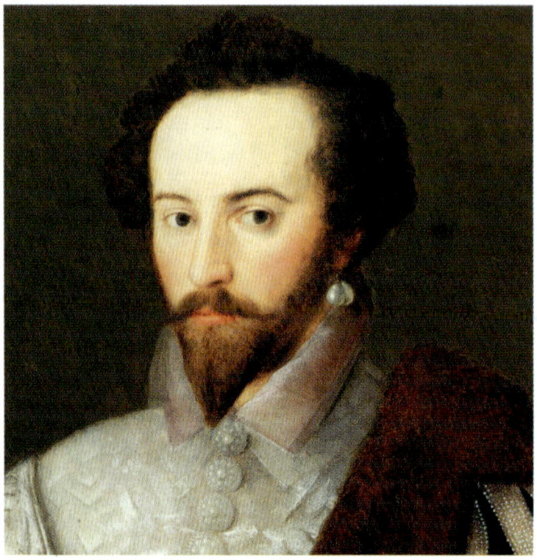

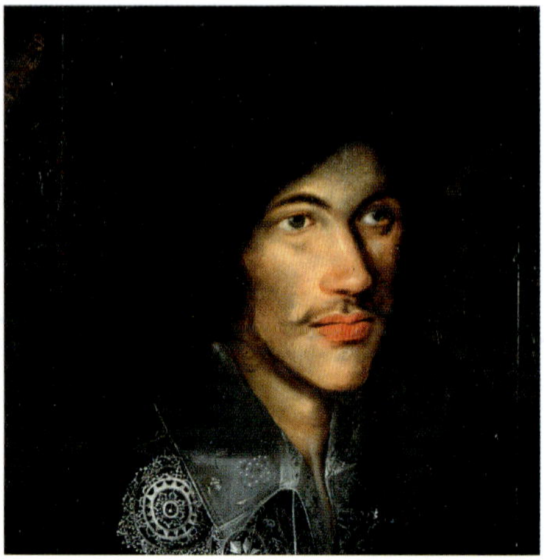

Details from the portraits of **Sir Walter Ralegh** (p.22) and **John Donne** (p.25)

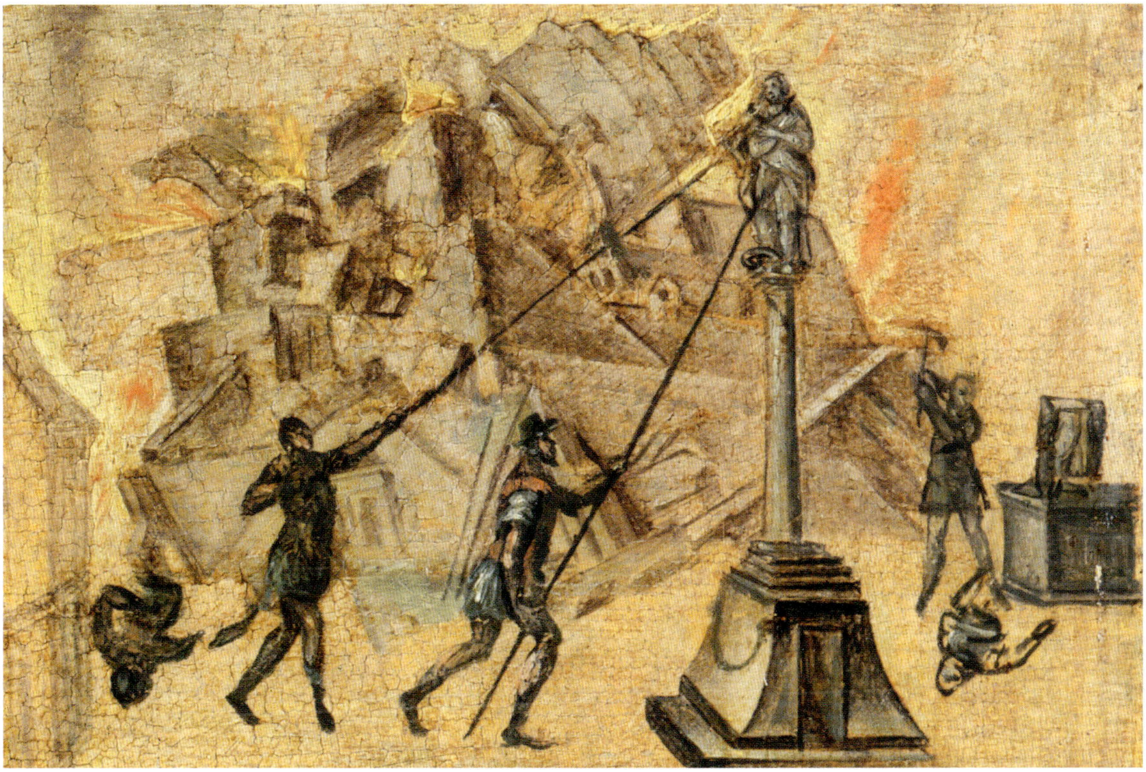

Detail from **Edward VI and the Pope**
Unknown artist, *c.*1570
Oil on panel,
622 x 908mm
(NPG 4165)

In this background scene, Protestant reformers are shown destroying religious icons.

Portraiture leaves its mark

Portraits survive in larger numbers than any other type of English painting from the 1500s, and their presence in country houses and museums dominates our understanding of what artists produced in this period. Yet, what exists today does not reflect the variety of imagery that was painted. At the time when portraiture was becoming popular, England was in a dramatic state of flux. During the reigns of Henry VIII and his children Edward VI, Mary I and Elizabeth I, England changed twice over from a Roman Catholic to a Protestant country. Many religious paintings were destroyed during the Reformation when Protestant reformers forcibly removed images from churches (above). During the civil wars in the mid seventeenth century religious pictures were also the target of the Puritans.

Many decorative paintings, which covered the walls of domestic interiors, have been destroyed along with the wooden houses they decorated. In addition, decorative imagery produced for temporary events, such as theatrical set designs and banners and often painted by the same artists who produced portraits, have also been lost.

The development of British portraiture 1500–1625

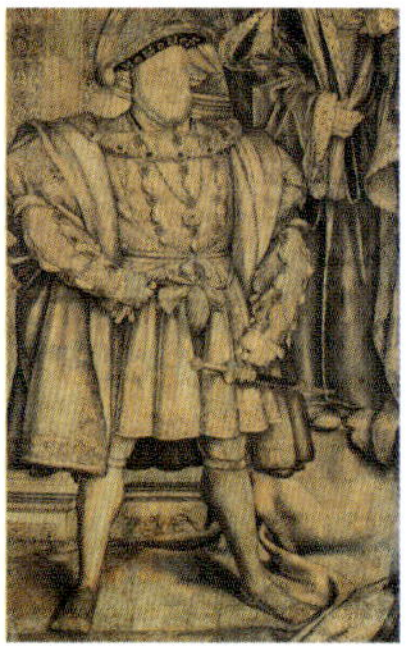

1500–30s Portraiture is a relatively new genre of painting in England and is principally restricted to members of the royal family and courtiers.

1526 Hans Holbein the Younger first arrives in England, one of many émigré artists who come to work for Henry VIII's court (pp.30–31).

1540s Portraits of wealthy English merchants and citizens outside the royal court begin to be painted.

1543 Holbein dies in England.

1500

1505 A portrait of Henry VII is painted and sent to Margaret of Savoy as part of a marriage proposal, possibly one of several portraits exchanged around this time (p.27).

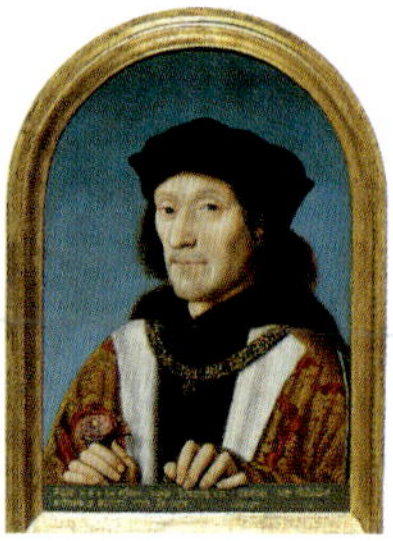

1536 Holbein paints a full-sized mural of Henry VIII and his family at Whitehall Palace (above left and p.30).

1547–53 During Edward VI's reign churches are required to remove paintings, and iconoclastic attacks on religious images take place. Consequently, artists mainly produce secular imagery (p.5).

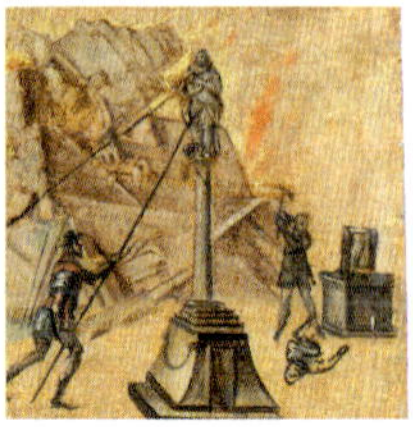

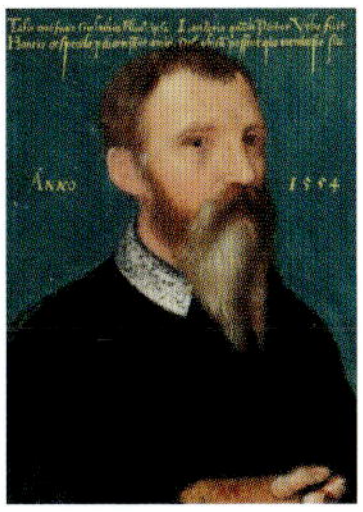

1554–5 Gerlach Flicke produces the first surviving self-portrait of an artist painted in England (p.42).

1568–70s A large influx of foreign artists arrives in England due to religious persecution in France and the southern Netherlands.

1572 Nicholas Hilliard paints his first portrait of Queen Elizabeth I (p.12, p.34).

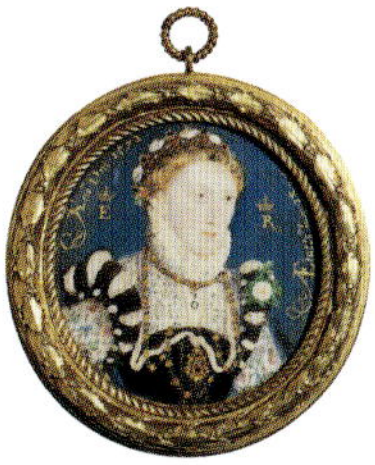

Late 1580s–90s Ruffs are at their largest. Throughout the period, fashion is an important indicator of the portrait's date (p.35).

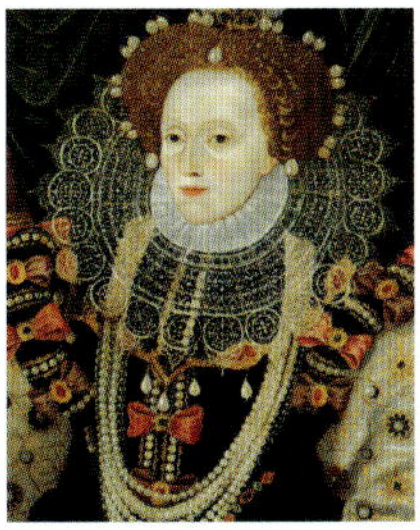

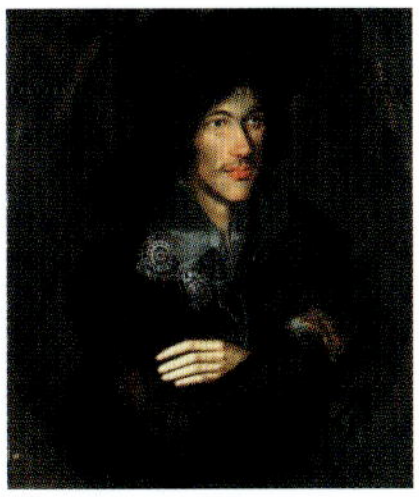

1590s Portraiture is increasingly employed by citizens (p.25).

1590s Canvas as a support for paintings comes into regular use alongside wooden panels.

1590s Sets of portraits of kings and queens become popular and are produced in quantities for display in the houses of the nobility and gentry (p.26).

1610s Group family portraits start to become more popular (p.41).

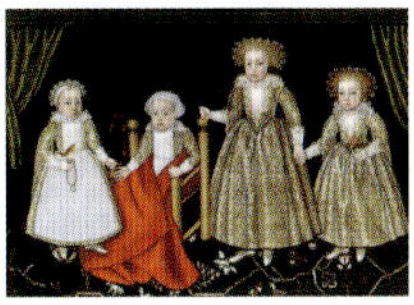

1625

Commissioning portraits

In the sixteenth century there were many different reasons for commissioning a portrait, and the functions of portraiture changed depending upon the status and circumstances of the sitter.

Loyalty and diplomacy

The reigning Tudor monarchs were more visible to their subjects than previous rulers, and ownership of their portraits showed loyalty to the crown.

Portraits of monarchs painted from life and displayed in royal palaces, or commissioned by important courtiers, often formed the basis for many other versions, which could be widely distributed. Many portraits of Elizabeth I were produced to support an expanding market, made up of courtiers and the nobility as well as members of the landowning classes and the urban élite.

In a diplomatic context, portraits of a reigning monarch and rulers of other countries were given or exchanged as a gesture of political friendship.

Marriage negotiations

For reigning monarchs the production of a new portrait might be linked to marriage negotiations (p.27). As the bride and groom might not have had the opportunity to meet before the wedding, the exchange of portraits allowed the various parties to consider the physical appearance and possible virtues of the prospective match.

Status, wealth and power

For courtiers and the nobility, portraiture was an important way of demonstrating their status, wealth and power, which could be indicated by dress, jewellery, coats of arms, emblems and symbols of honour and office, as well as by employing the most accomplished foreign painters (p.42). Historically, the nobility often won their titles as a reward for military service to the crown, and portraiture could also represent acts of heroism or celebrate military victories. As in the portrait of Sir Edward Hoby (p.21), many noblemen were shown in armour with a helmet alongside, which might represent either actual participation in military action or the willingness to serve.

Recording likeness

One of the essential functions of portraiture for sitters from all backgrounds was to record physical likeness for family, friends and loved ones, as well as for posterity. As one contemporary observer commented, portraits were a useful way to see 'how time doth alter them'. For this reason, individuals might commission several portraits of themselves at different times of their lives. For example, there are at least twelve surviving portraits of Robert Dudley, Earl of Leicester (p.16) painted in his lifetime. The same commentator added that for later descendants portraits were a useful way to see the 'manner of favour', or the character and likeness of their forebears. After the sitter's death, a portrait could become a type of memorial.

Since portraits could be produced in multiple copies (which today can cause confusion about which, if any, is the original version) different branches of a family could display portraits of family members and close friends, reinforcing family and wider community connections.

Rites of passage

For the gentry and private citizens, portraits were also produced to record particular rites of passage, such as marriage (for example, the marriage of Lady Scudamore's son, p.18), death (see Sir Henry Unton's portrait, pp.24–5), or another important event in the life of the sitter, such as the award of honours or appointment to a new political post.

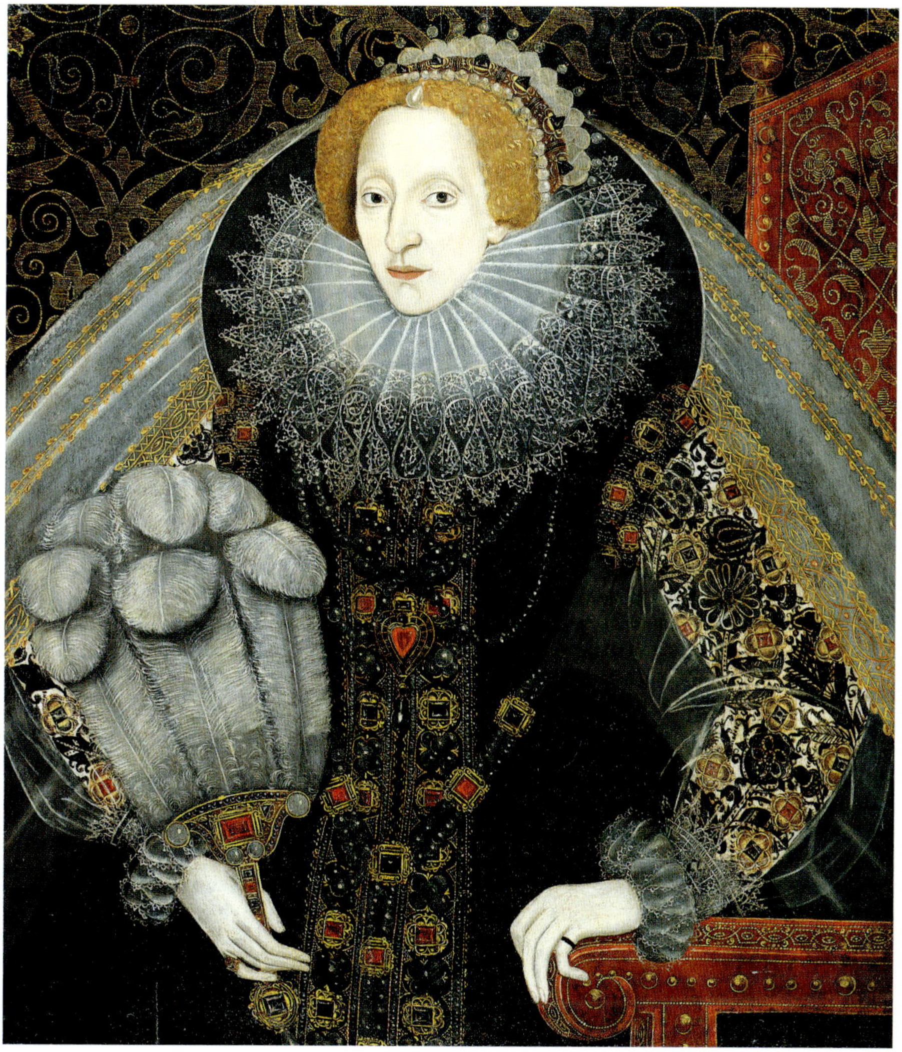

Elizabeth I
Unknown artist, *c.*1585–90
Oil on panel, 953 x 819mm
(NPG 2471)

Portraits of the Queen were popular and could be purchased both ready made or by commission. This portrait was found in a seventeenth-century farmhouse in 1890. It is one of a standard type, which exists in several other versions.

Owning and displaying portraits

In contrast to the very high cost of clothes, jewellery and household goods, such as tapestries, musical instruments and large-scale items of furniture, painted portraits were relatively inexpensive. Prices would vary considerably depending on the skill of the artist, the size of the portrait and the complexity of the composition, but it was certainly possible for middle-class and modestly wealthy individuals to afford their own portraits.

Who owned portraits?
By the second half of the sixteenth century, the fashion for portraiture had spread from the court to more ordinary people, including artists, writers, merchants and professional men. Surviving inventories of Tudor and Jacobean households occasionally list portraits and provide valuations. The lack of a flourishing art market and the personal nature of portraiture, with its limited resale possibilities, meant that these valuations were often quite low. Occasionally they might be as little as sixpence, but more typically paintings were valued between one and five shillings (roughly the price of a cheap Bible in the period 1560–80 or an item of luxury foodstuffs, such as a jar of olives, around 1600). New portraits probably cost more to commission, typically around ten to twenty shillings; however, courtiers who employed distinguished artists (p.42), such as Hans Holbein the Younger, would pay considerably more.

Where were portraits displayed?
Portraiture was a relatively new genre in Tudor England and for much of the sixteenth century portraits were principally on display in royal palaces and in the houses of nobility.

By around 1600, however, portraits were displayed in a number of different places, including university dining halls, town halls, guild or livery company halls, and also as signage outside shops and inns. Of course, portraits of the monarch also appeared on the coinage found in everyone's pockets and purses. Private individuals who commissioned their own portraits would hang the framed panels in their own homes – often in the main room of the house or the bedroom.

Members of the nobility and gentry with large country estates also took to building long galleries at the top of their houses; many of these were used to display pictures of family members and sets of English monarchs (p.26) and other worthies. The existing long galleries at Montacute House in Somerset and Hardwick Hall in Derbyshire remain two of the most impressive.

Long gallery, Montacute House, *c.*1600

Today, the display of pictures in the long gallery at Montacute House is influenced by conservation concerns about light levels, and most of the pictures are shown in the side rooms adjoining the long gallery.

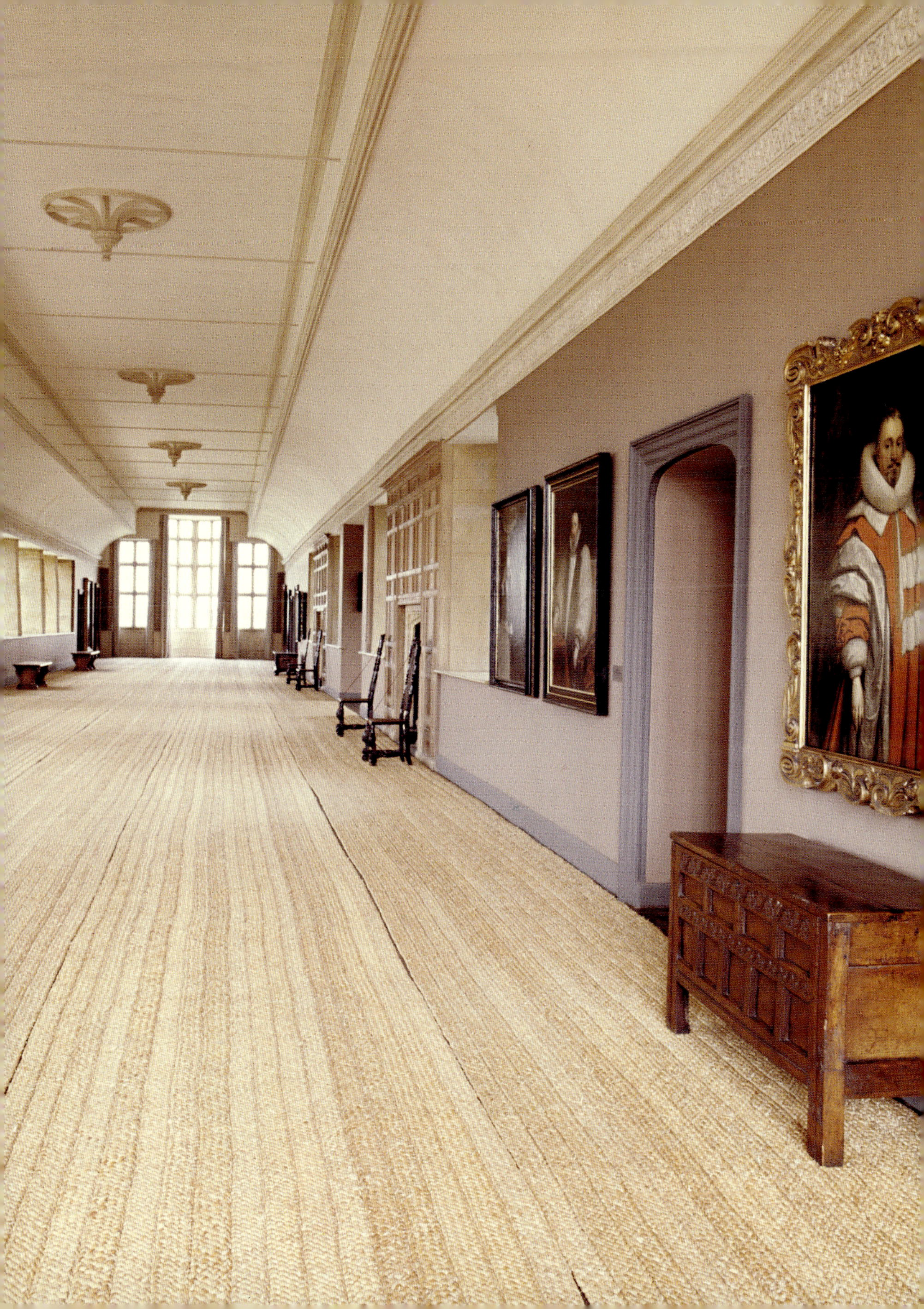

Portrait formats

Tudor and Jacobean portraits were produced in various sizes, according to the patron's taste and pocket. When making a choice, patrons would visit artists' studios, and here they would have been inspired by other formats and designs.

Portrait size and scale

Most portraits produced at this time were life-sized images, which were designed to create a dynamic illusion of actual presence. A common contemporary term for a portrait was 'counterfeit', which reflects this idea of a duplicated likeness of the living sitter. Full-length portraiture was first used to portray monarchs, but by the late sixteenth century full-length portraits were increasingly popular with courtiers and the gentry. This coincided with the use of canvas rather than wooden panels, which allowed large-scale paintings to be produced more easily.

Smaller head-and-shoulders or half-length portraits were more portable, less labour intensive and for the patron, cheaper than larger images. Even with this smaller size it was common for the artist to work to scale.

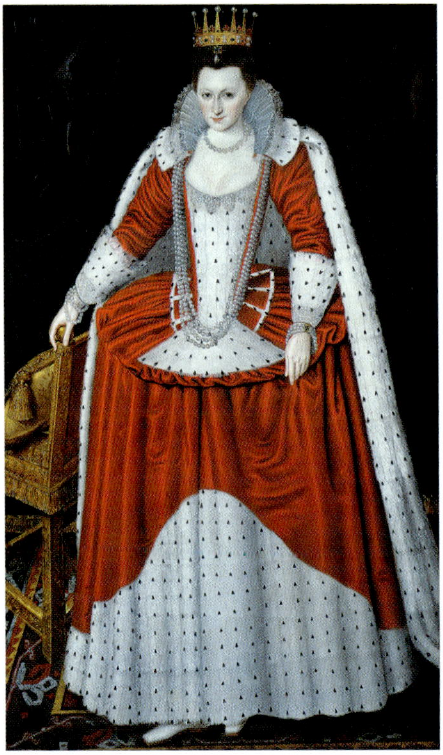

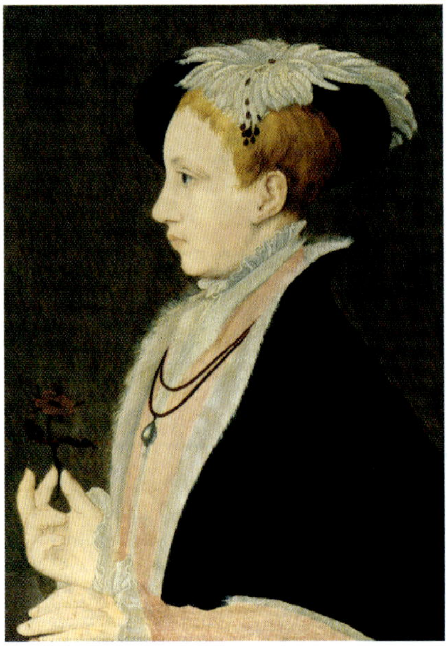

Far left: **Possibly Lucy, Countess of Bedford** (*c.*1581–1627)
Unknown artist, *c.*1603
Oil on panel,
1914 x 1138mm
(NPG 5688)

Left: **Edward VI** (1537–53)
By an artist in the studio of William Scrots (active 1537–53), *c.*1546
Oil on panel,
473 x 279mm
(NPG 442)

Below: **Elizabeth I** (1533–1603)
Nicholas Hilliard (1547?–*c.*1619), 1572
Watercolour on vellum,
oval 51 x 48mm
(NPG 108)

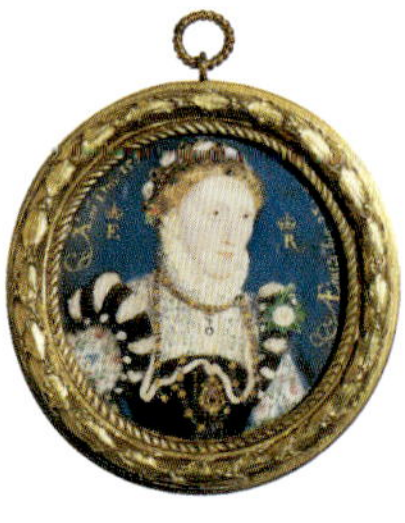

Miniatures formed another category of portraiture; these small-scale images tended to have a more personal function. They were popular with courtiers and were often set into elaborate jewelled cases with covers. Miniatures could be worn around the neck, pinned to clothing or secretly concealed on the body as way of honouring the memory of a loved one.

Inscriptions and heraldic symbols

Painted inscriptions and heraldic symbols are common features of Tudor and Jacobean portraiture and were usually suggested to the artist by the sitter. The inscriptions frequently record the sitter's age, the date at which the portrait was painted or specific sentiments or mottos written either in English or Latin. An inscription pinpointing the age of the sitter enhances the portrait's role as a documentary record of likeness. Inscriptions often disrupt the illusion of representation, but British patrons were usually more concerned with recording a moment in time than with artistic illusion.

Coats of arms were designed above all to proclaim the status of the sitters and their family lineage or recently acquired honours.

Details from the portrait of **Sir Edward Hoby** (p.21)

Right: the top line of writing above the coat of arms shows the date the portrait was painted, and the second line shows the age of the sitter.

Above far right: the woman holds a banner with a Latin inscription, translated as 'laid aside but not blunted'.

Below far right: the baton by Hoby's side is inscribed with the Latin text, translated at 'anger without strength is vain'.

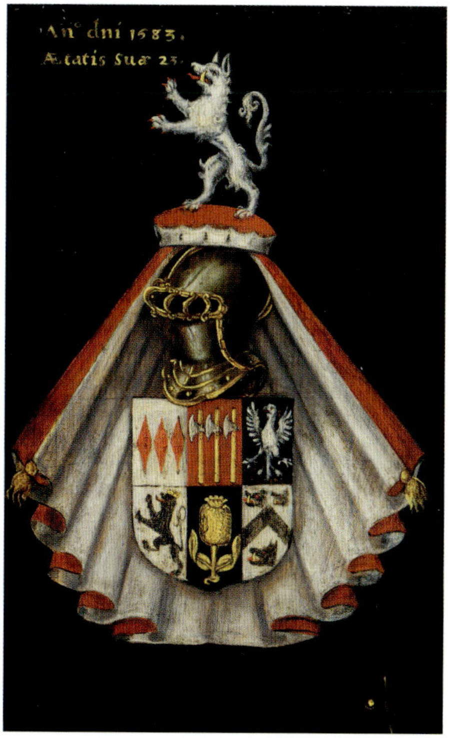

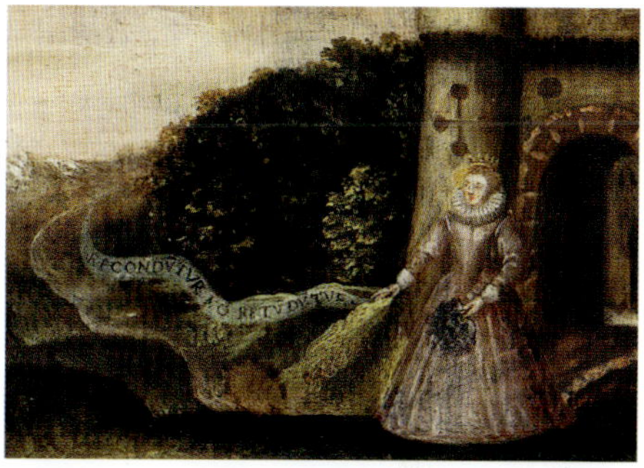

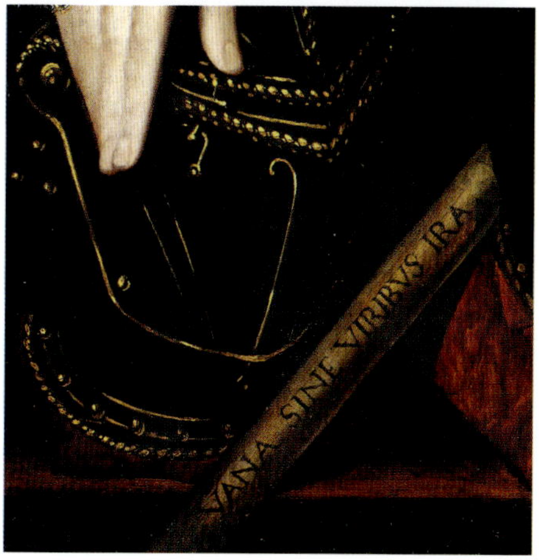

Costume and portraiture

The clothing a person wore was seen as a true reflection of his or her status in life. Textiles and tailoring were extremely expensive, and items of clothing were often the most costly and prized possessions of Tudor nobility. It was even possible to move up the social ladder by wearing expensive clothes, and by the 1550s England had become known in Europe as the place where a man's clothes, rather than his birth, defined the status of a 'gentleman'. Men dressed as flamboyantly as women in the Tudor and Jacobean periods.

As today, fashions changed quickly. This was particularly true for wealthier members of society who were keen to be painted in their most fashionable outfits. As a result it is often possible to date a portrait to within five or ten years by identifying the fashion. In the early Tudor period men's costume was characterised by an exaggerated masculinity, with wide shoulders tapering to narrow hips and a padded codpiece as seen in the portrait of Henry VIII (p.30). During the later Elizabethan period courtly dress for men and women had an overblown, dramatic quality, which distorted the shape of the body. The ruff, which had begun as a frilled edge to a shirt, had become a separate accessory. With the introduction of starch in the 1560s, the ruff grew larger and by the late sixteenth century, it had become the most striking feature, as in the 'Armada' portrait of Elizabeth I (p.34).

Catherine Parr (1512–48)

This portrait of Henry VIII's sixth and last wife provides good examples of both the style and the components of a high-ranking woman's costume in the early Tudor period. The rich colours and fabrics adorned with pearls, gold and silver thread; her sumptuous lynx fur sleeves; and the elaborate array of jewels all indicate the sitter's wealth and status. The crown-headed brooch pinned to her dress appears in a surviving inventory of Catherine Parr's jewels. The wide square neckline was fashionable at this date and shows off her pale and delicate skin tone.

Detail from the portrait of **Catherine Parr** (right) This highly magnified section shows where the outerskirt meets the underskirt. The outerskirt is lined with fur and the white diagonal lines represent the individual hairs of fur poking out from the edge. The artist used silver leaf beneath the red areas to make the underskirt more lustrous.

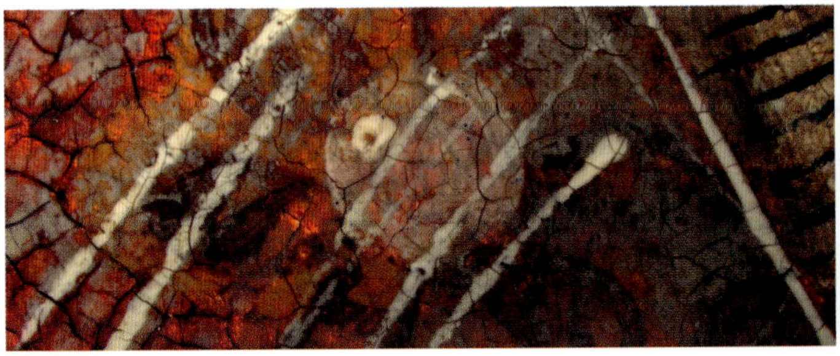

Catherine Parr
Attributed to Master John (active 1544–*c*.50), *c*.1545
Oil on panel,
1803 x 940mm
(NPG 4451)

Sir Henry Lee
Antonis Mor (1516/20–76?), 1568
Oil on panel,
641 x 533mm
(NPG 2095)

Sir Henry Lee (1533–1611)

The portraits of Elizabethan courtiers frequently include items of costume and jewellery that were designed to show loyalty to the Queen, such as miniatures or cameos with her portrait. This portrait of the courtier Sir Henry Lee employs subtle and complex allusions to Elizabeth I and demonstrates the symbolic importance attached to costume at her court. Lee wears the Queen's personal colours of white, gold, red and black and his sleeves are decorated with armillary spheres – an emblem associated with Elizabeth I – and lovers' knots. Who the painting was commissioned for and whether the Queen ever saw it is not known. The meanings of the three gold rings tied onto red cord and worn at his wrist and upper arm and held by his thumb on his chest cannot be easily explained. The gesture would seem to indicate an offer of love and devotion, either to the Queen or to a lover. Each viewer may have interpreted it differently.

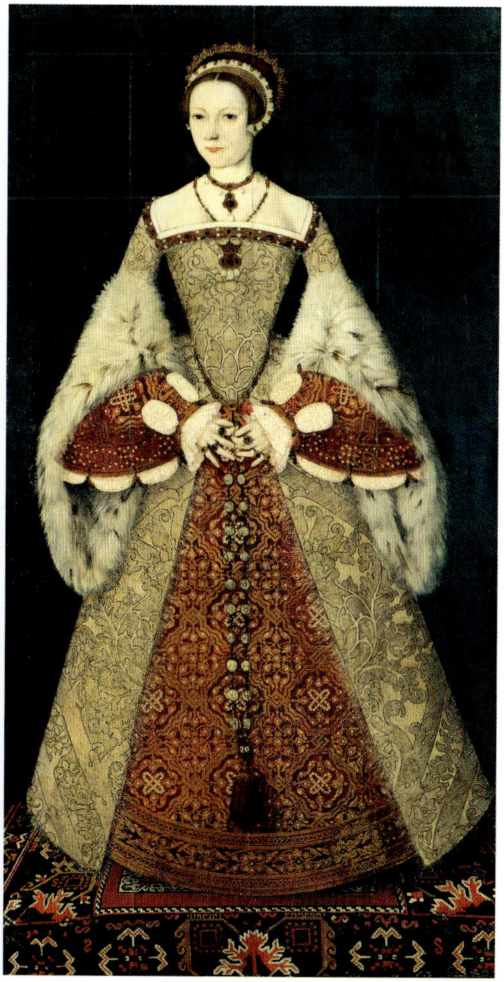

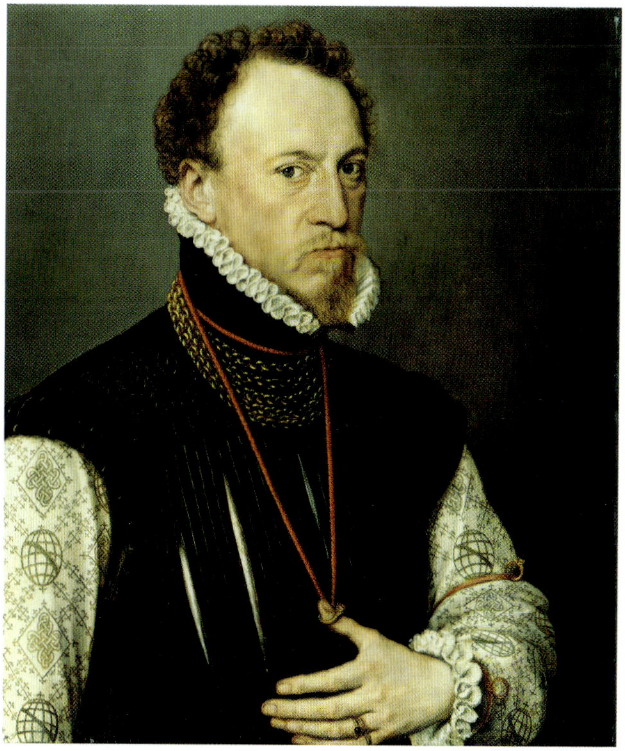

Robert Dudley, Earl of Leicester (1532–88)
Leicester, Elizabeth I's most famous and influential favourite, was noted for taking particular interest in his appearance. He is seen here in a red silk or satin suit lavishly embroidered with gold thread and he wears a matching red feather in his jewelled cap. His moustache and beard are fashionably styled for the 1570s. Dress for men in the Elizabethan period was more effeminate than in the previous generation, better suited to dancing and the chivalric rituals of courtly life dominated by a queen. The large codpiece favoured under Henry VIII had all but disappeared and the hose (short trousers) became shorter, revealing the wearer's shapely legs clad in silk stockings.

Elizabeth Knollys, Lady Layton
Elizabeth Knollys had a special interest in clothes and accessories as she was almost certainly the person who had day-to-day care of Elizabeth I's fabulous wardrobe. As a Maid of Honour she appeared alongside the Queen at chapel and at court events. The Queen's ladies occasionally received items from the royal wardrobe, which could be very valuable. In 1565 for example, Elizabeth Knollys was given a 'Venetian gown of crimson velvet'. Her own costume, shown here, is extremely elaborate. Her jewellery includes rubies, pearls and probably jets or diamonds, and her tall black hat is adorned with pearls. Striking feathers and jewelled hat badges were highly fashionable at this date.

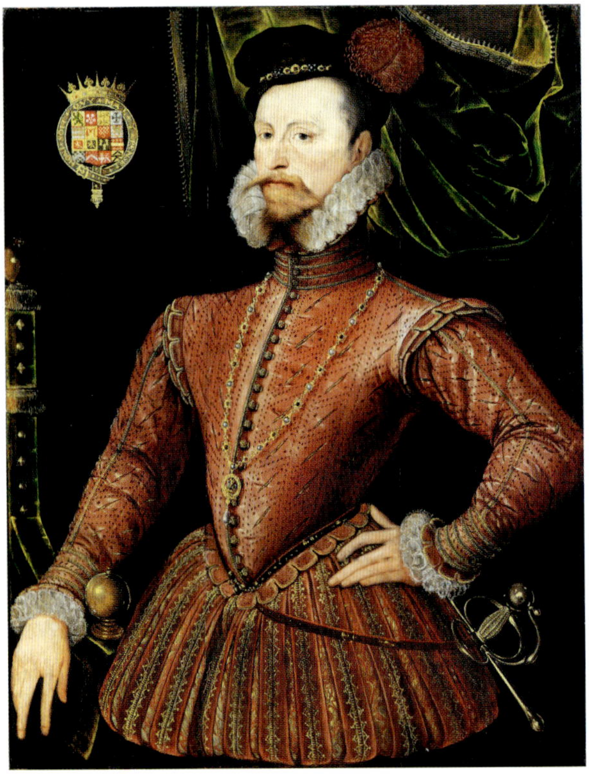

Robert Dudley, Earl of Leicester
Unknown artist, *c.*1575
Oil on panel,
1080 x 826mm
(NPG 447)

Elizabeth Knollys, Lady Layton
Attributed to George Gower (*c.*1540–96), *c.*1577
Oil on panel,
610 x 705mm
Montacute House
(The National Trust)

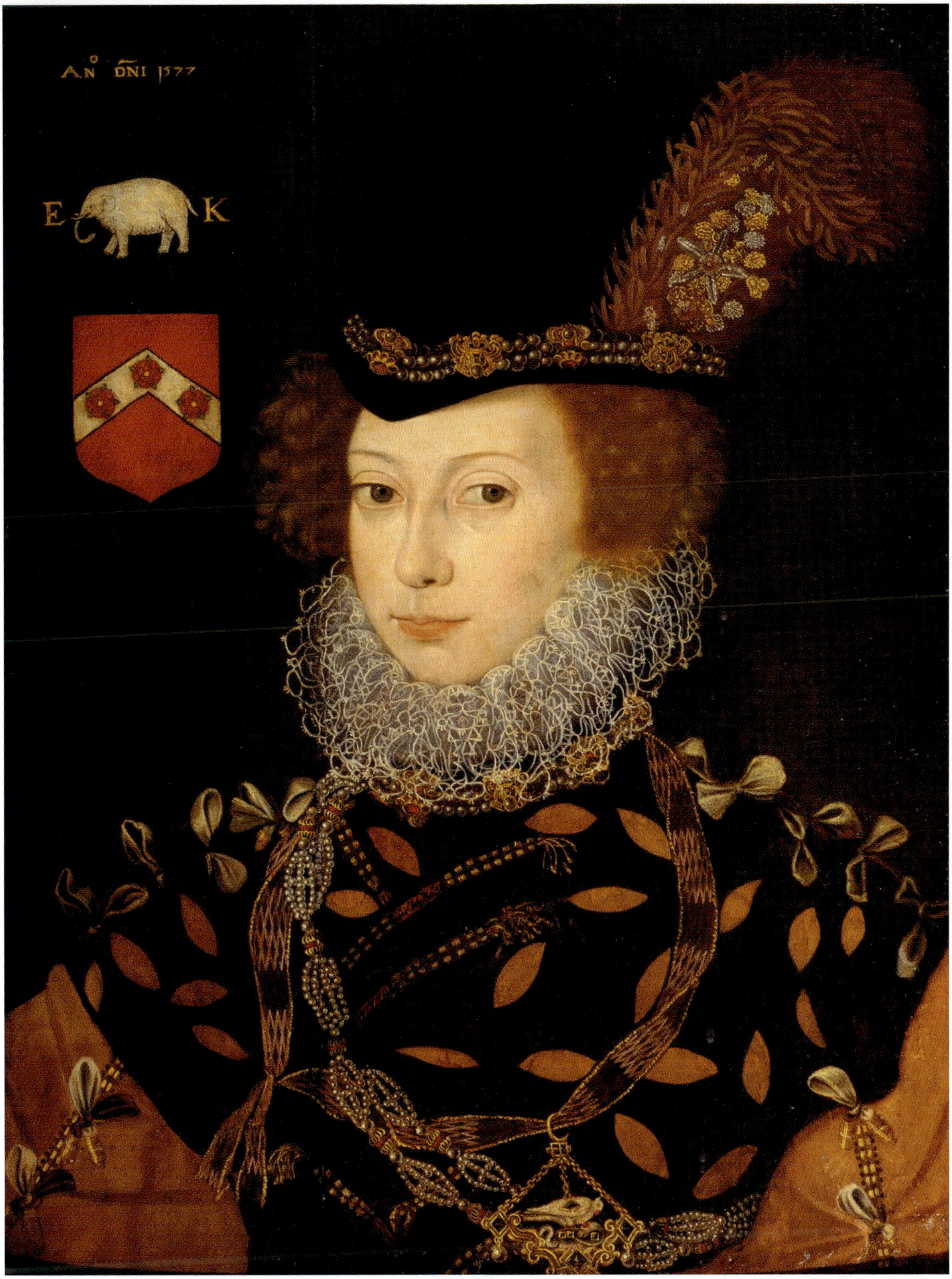
E K

Mary Throckmorton, Lady Scudamore (d.1632)

The red, black and white colour scheme and the startlingly lavish detail of this costume were designed to impress its original viewers and to create an impression of a middle-aged woman still at the height of her powers. She is shown wearing richly embroidered fashionable clothes with one hand tucked into the folds of her coat, which is lined with fur for warmth. The artist Marcus Gheeraerts the Younger was exceptionally talented at capturing the translucency of skin and floating lace, the subtleties of the Jacobean floral embroidery and the surface texture and weight of brocaded fabrics falling around the body.

The portrait commemorates the marriage of Lady Scudamore's son, John (later Viscount Scudamore), with the date it took place inscribed at the top right, surrounded by a floral wreath and the words 'no spring 'till now'. The marriage offered hope that the Scudamore family lineage would be preserved. The elaborate array of three different floral designs, shown on her doublet (a tightly fitted jacket), coat and skirt complement this theme of the promise of new life.

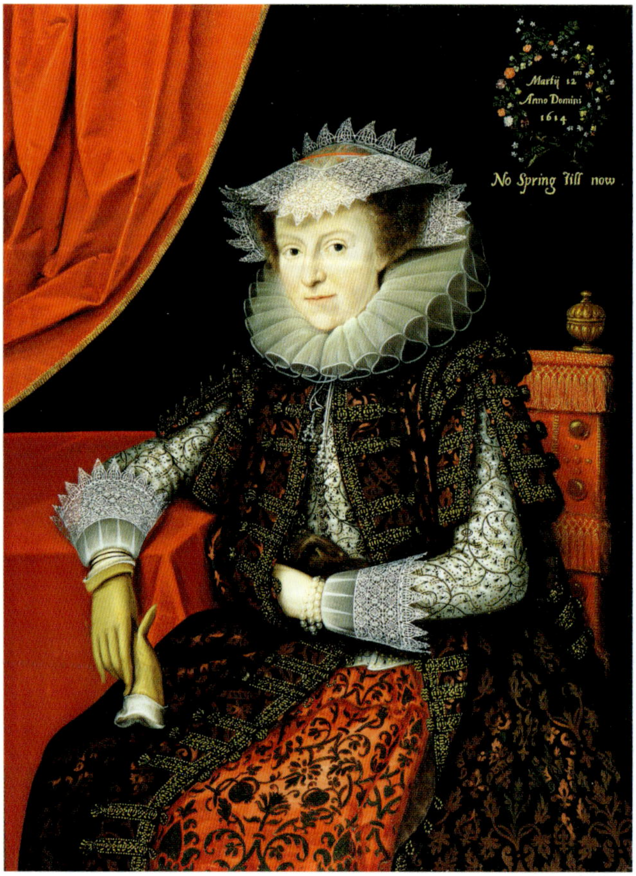

Mary Throckmorton, Lady Scudamore
Marcus Gheeraerts the Younger (1561–1635/6), 1615
Oil on panel, 1143 x 826mm
(NPG 64)

Anne of Denmark
Unknown artist,
after Paul Van Somer
(1577/8–1621/2), *c.*1617
Oil on canvas,
629 x 533mm
(NPG 127)

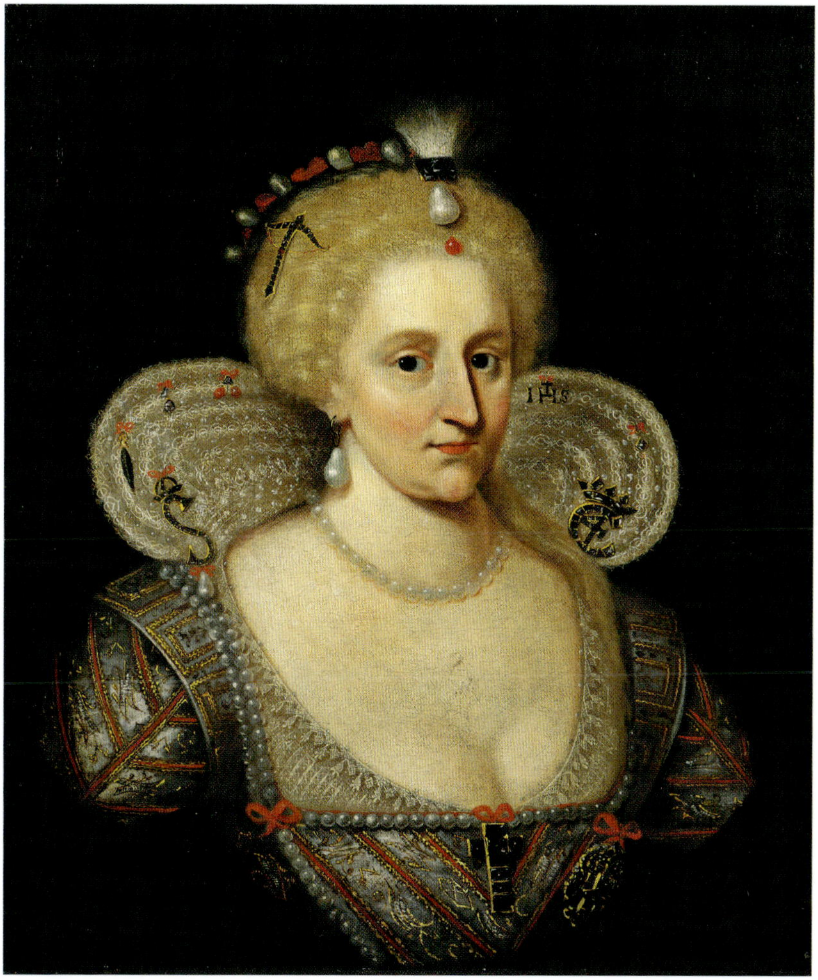

Anne of Denmark (1574–1619)
Jewellery was an essential part of the image of the royal family and courtiers. Portraits of Anne of Denmark, wife of James I, reveal a fondness for jewelled adornments, and she is shown here wearing some of the most famous and distinctive jewels from her spectacular collection. Tudor and Jacobean jewels were frequently crafted into heraldic emblems, animals or letters. Those worn by Anne refer to her immediate royal relations: the crowned 'S' pinned to the left side of her collar refers to her mother Sophia of Mecklenberg, and the crowned 'C' on the right to her brother Christian IV of Denmark. The distinctive crossbow-shaped jewel in her hair may have previously belonged to Elizabeth I, whose jewels were being distributed and sold off around this time. She also wears a jewelled sacred 'IHS' monogram and a large cross, symbols of the Catholic faith to which she had converted.

Pictures with stories to tell

Unravelling all the stories Tudor paintings had to tell their original audiences would be an impossible task today. Many of the symbols are difficult to interpret fully and their meanings, perhaps connected to specific contemporary events and personal relationships, are now lost to the modern viewer. Most educated Elizabethans would have read Latin and would have been able to translate the Latin mottos inscribed on portraits. However, simple translation was never the same as understanding, and the meaning of some mottos was purposefully obscure. These types of features point to the private use of portraiture as a tool for communicating and sharing personal illusions between friends, lovers, groups of intellectuals or associates.

At the court of Elizabeth I, courtiers were required to engage in a game of absolute devotion to the Queen. At court masques and other formal entertainments courtiers competed with each other to find complex, witty and inventive ways to demonstrate their loyalty, and some portraits like the picture of Walter Ralegh (p.22) retell these narratives. Portraits can also offer a view of a person as he or she wished to be seen, and therefore largely tell the story of an individual from their own perspective. But occasionally portraits were commissioned by a friend or spouse, as in the case of the portrait of Henry Unton (p.24), which was probably painted at the request of his widow.

Sir Edward Hoby (1560–1617)

The young Edward Hoby was a renowned soldier and scholar and both these roles are on display in this puzzling portrait, which shows him dressed in striking armour with a sword, baton and helmet. This picture certainly had a story to tell its original audience, though its exact meanings are no longer clear. The baton by Hoby's side is inscribed with Latin text, which can be translated as 'anger without strength is vain' perhaps referring to the futility of harbouring resentment without the ability to act. The meaning of the narrative scene shown through a window to the right of the figure is also difficult to interpret. The allegorical image seems to relate to a temporary pause in military action, as it shows a woman in front of a castle with discarded weapons and military trophies covered by a veil in the foreground. She holds a banner with a Latin inscription, which can be translated as 'laid aside but not blunted'.

From what we know of Hoby's activities in 1583, he was not involved in military action and this picture may have been designed to indicate his readiness to serve.

Sir Edward Hoby
Unknown artist, 1583
Oil on panel,
953 x 756mm
(NPG 1974)

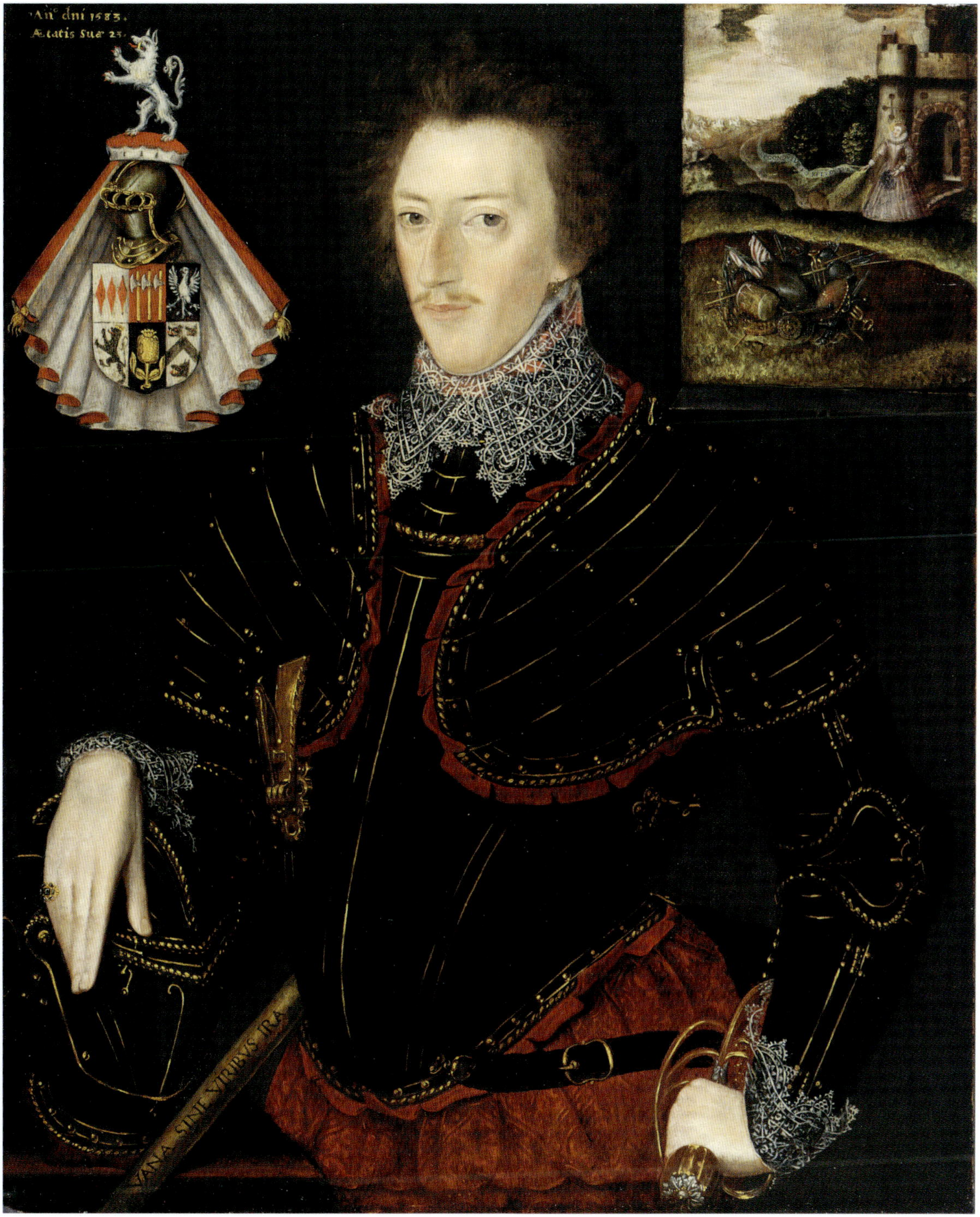
Anᵒ dni 1583.
Ætatis Suæ 23.
VANA SINE VIRIBVS IRA

Sir Walter Ralegh (1554–1618)
Ralegh's good looks, wit, literary skills, courtly manners and early success in maritime adventures created significant influence at court, yet he was alternately in and out of favour with the Queen. He presents himself here as the Queen's devoted servant. Although we do not know where the portrait originally hung, the picture was certainly designed to convey Ralegh's absolute loyalty to the Queen.

His costume is lavishly embroidered with valuable pearls, which as symbols of purity showed his admiration for Elizabeth, the 'Virgin Queen'. Ralegh also wears some of the Queen's personal colours of black and white, and the pattern of his cloak depicts the rays of the sun or the moon, an emblem associated with Elizabeth. At the top left, above a Latin inscription meaning 'by love and virtue', is a crescent moon: a device that perhaps refers to Ralegh's own poetry in praise of the Queen, which compares her with Cynthia, the Moon Goddess.

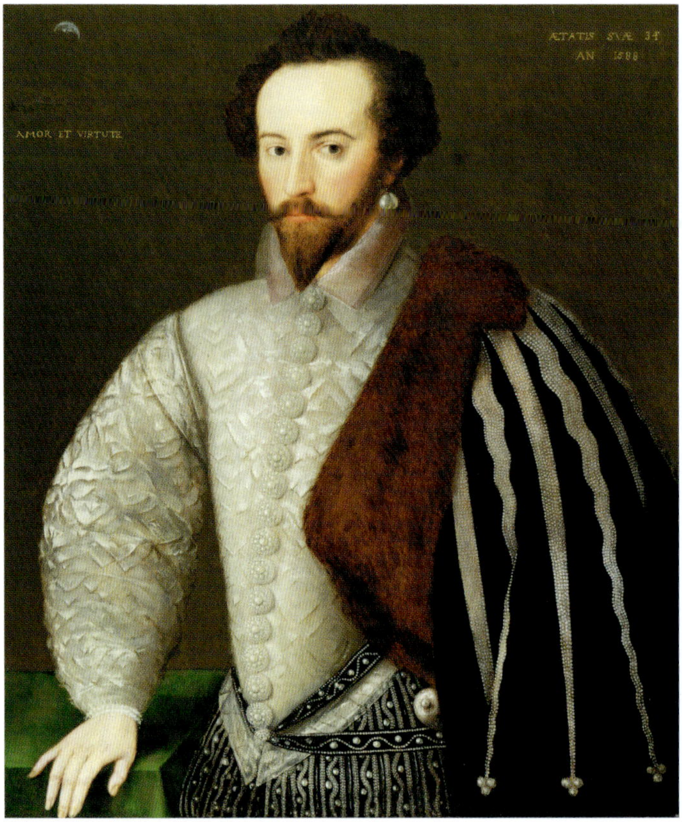

Sir John Luttrell (1518?–51)
One of a handful of allegorical portraits produced in the Tudor period, this image of a naked man wading in the sea depicts the courtier and soldier Sir John Luttrell. The picture demonstates Luttrell's role as a warrior and his courage and constancy in the face of danger. A wrecked English ship, flying a flag with the cross of St George, appears to the right and in the sky is the figure of Peace holding an olive branch in her hand. The content was probably designed to celebrate Luttrell's role in events around 1550, following the Treaty of Boulogne, which brought to an end the war between England, France and Scotland. Luttrell, while fighting in Scotland, was taken prisoner, but the English government paid for his ransom.

This picture was painted for George Luttrell, Sir John's nephew and heir and the original version (now in poor condition) dating from the 1550s is at the Courtauld Institute Gallery, London.

Above: **Sir Walter Ralegh**
Attributed to the Monogramist 'H' (active 1588), 1588
Oil on panel,
914 x 746mm
(NPG 7)

Opposite: **Allegorical portrait of Sir John Luttrell**
After Hans Eworth (active 1540–74), 1591
Oil on panel,
1110 x 825mm
Dunster Castle
(The National Trust)

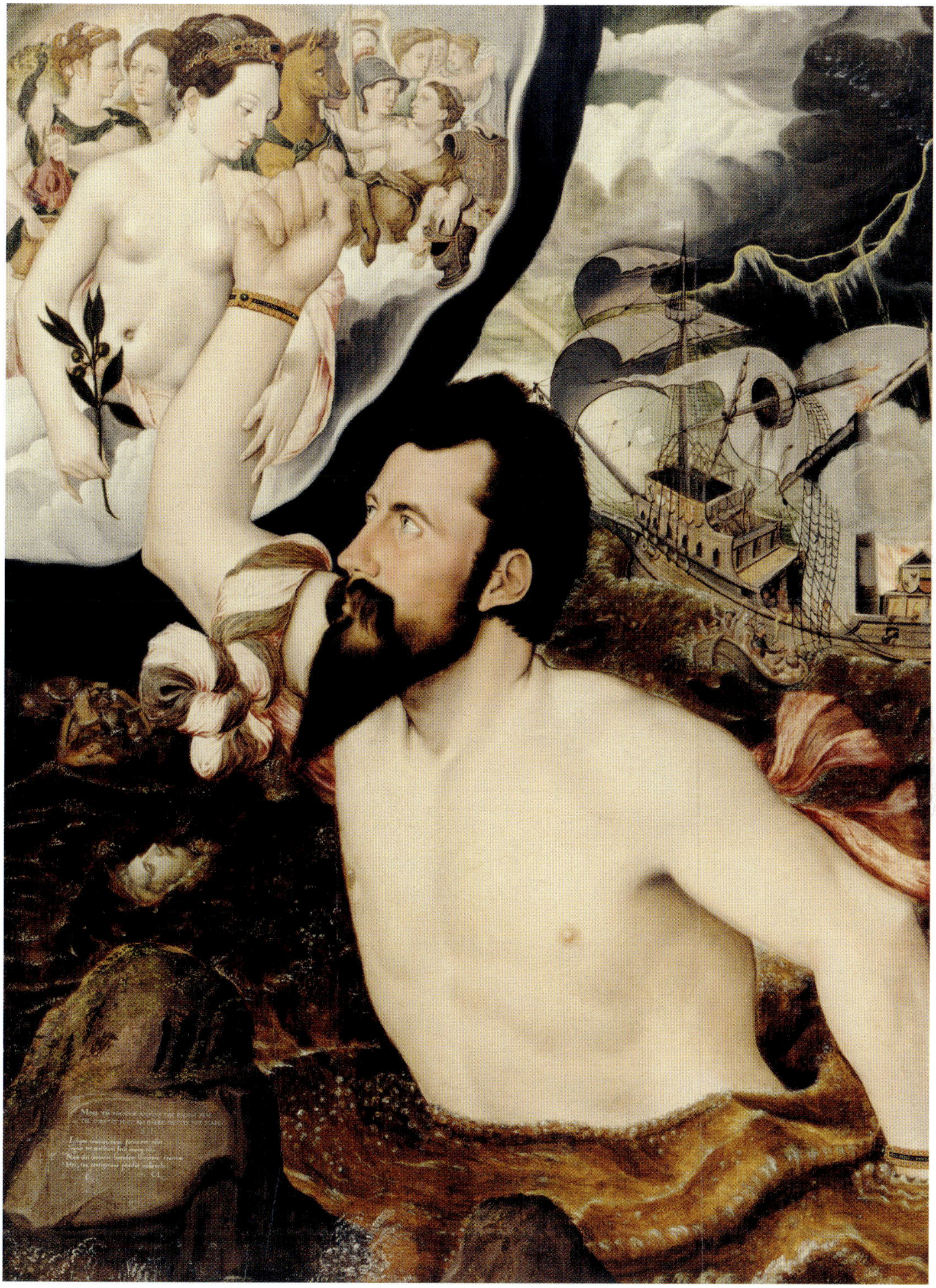

Sir Henry Unton (c.1558–96)
This painting tells the story of the life and death of the Elizabethan soldier and diplomat Henry Unton. This type of English narrative painting is highly unusual and Unton is portrayed at least ten times in various scenes from his life and death.

The action is arranged in a magazine-like style with small consecutive scenes painted around three dominant features: Unton's portrait (centre), his house near Oxford (right) and the church where he was buried (left). The story begins at the bottom right corner where we see Unton as a baby in his mother's arms, and then above studying at Oxford University and travelling abroad in Italy – the word 'venis' [Venice] is marked top right. This is followed to the left by his military service in the Low Countries and his deathbed in France. The long funeral procession, with its file of sombre mourners dressed in black moving towards the church, takes up most of the lower half of the painting.

This idiosyncratic portrait was probably commissioned by his widow Dorothy after Sir Henry Unton's death in 1596 as an elaborate memorial to his achievements.

Sir Henry Unton
Unknown artist, c.1596
Oil on panel,
740 x 1632mm
(NPG 710)

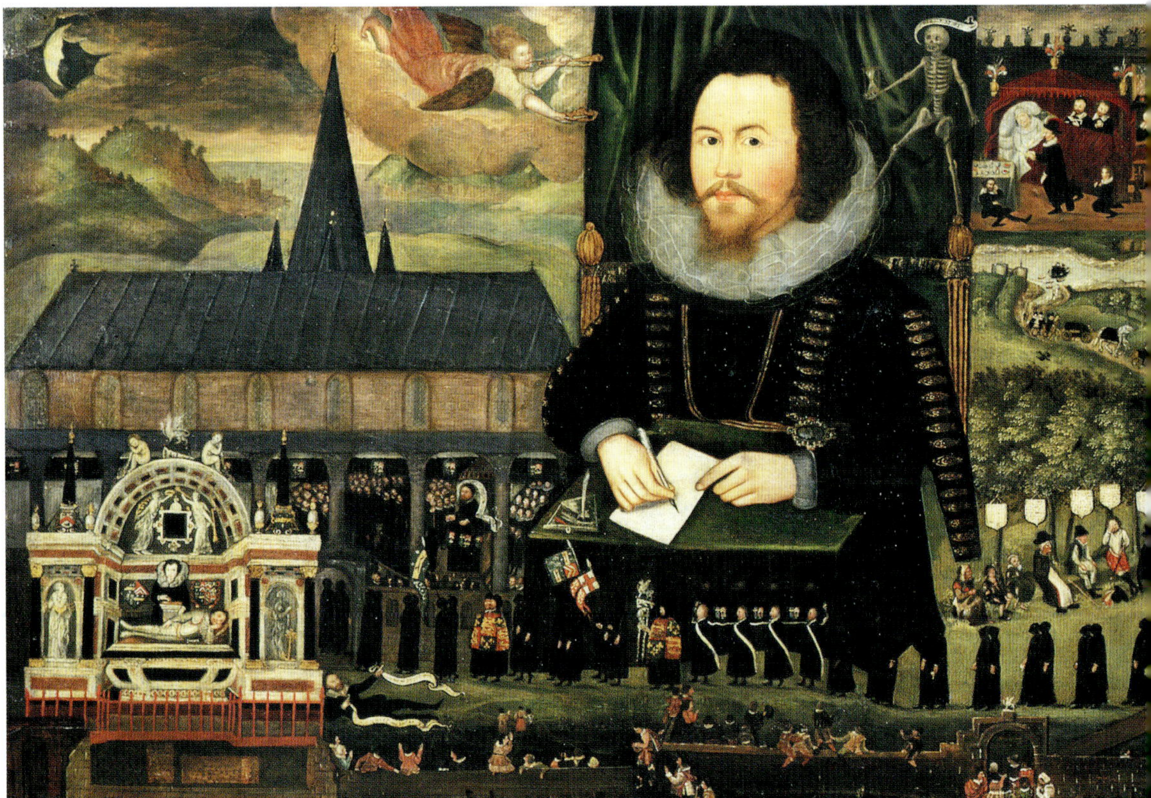

John Donne
Unknown English artist, *c.*1595
Oil on panel,
771 x 625mm
(NPG 6790)

John Donne (*c.*1572–1631)

One of the earliest images of an Elizabethan poet, this portrait of the exceptionally talented John Donne was perhaps designed as a personal message to an unknown lover. The portrait may reflect Donne's troubled heart and his melancholy state of mind when, as a young man in his early twenties, he was finishing his education at the Inns of Court in London.

Donne is shown here in an unusual pose with his head set back in shadows, his collar untied and arms crossed, as if caught up in contemplation. The Latin inscription around the edge of the oval can be translated as 'O Lady lighten our darkness' and might be read as a plea to a reluctant lover.

Donne was probably closely involved in the composition, and this important portrait has been described as a product of his imagination, 'as much as the Elegies and Satires'. Donne described the portrait in his own will as 'the picture of myne which is taken in the shaddowes' when he bequeathed it to a friend just before his death.

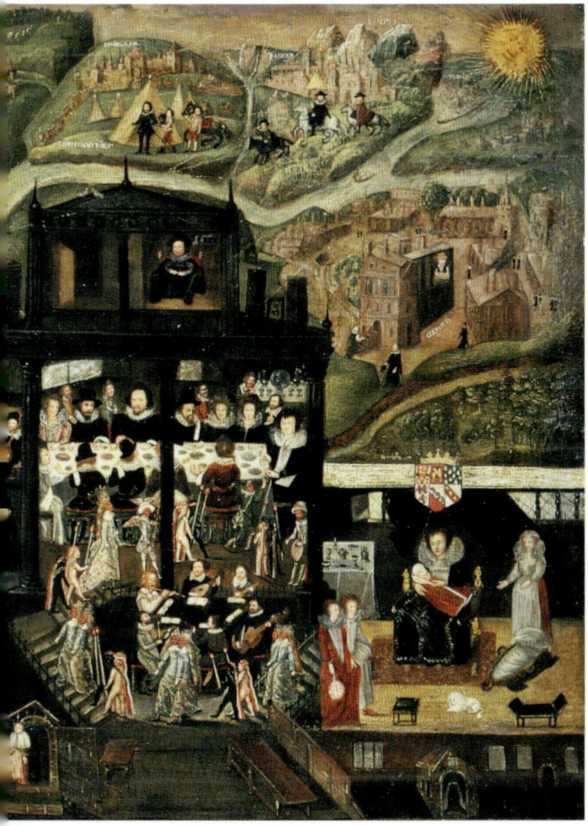

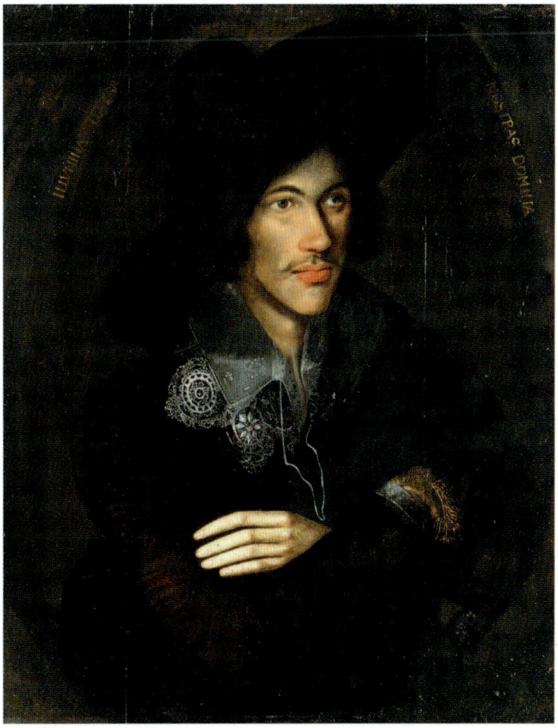

The monarchy

Images of the reigning monarch and of his or her predecessors made up a large proportion of the portraits produced in this period. As sittings from life were rarely granted, most surviving Tudor and Jacobean royal portraits are versions of existing types, which were then copied from approved patterns. The considerable numbers of portraits of Henry VIII and Elizabeth I that exist today reflect not simply their long reigns, but the importance of the royal portrait as a symbol of loyalty at a time of significant religious and political turmoil.

Towards the end of the sixteenth century, it became fashionable to acquire sets of portraits of past kings and queens.

The Hornby Castle set of kings and queens
These portraits of monarchs from William the Conqueror to Mary I presented a remarkable display of visual history and continuity. This set used to hang at Hornby Castle in Yorkshire and may have been commissioned for a long gallery. While some of the portraits were based on existing images, such as Richard III, they were frequently based on imaginary sources popularised by books on the history of Britain printed in the late 1500s and early 1600s.

Although these sets were probably quite popular at the time, only a few survive intact today. Examples can be seen at Montacute House and Hardwick Hall.

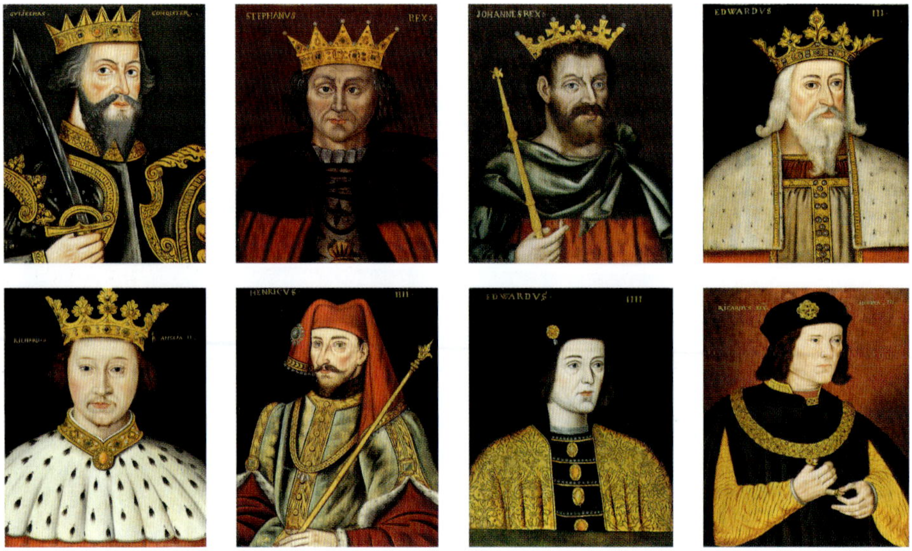

Eight of sixteen portraits from the Hornby Castle set of kings and queens: William I, Stephen, John, Edward III, Richard II, Henry IV, Edward IV and Richard III
Unknown English artists, late sixteenth or early seventeenth century
Oil on panel, approx. 580 x 450mm each
(NPG 4980: 1, 2, 3, 5, 7, 8, 10, 12)

This amusing set of kings and queens was painted in at least two separate groups, the Tudor monarchs and Richard III in the period 1595–1605, and the earlier kings in the 1620s.

Henry VII (1457–1509)

This compelling portrait of Henry VII, the founder of the Tudor dynasty, was painted as part of marriage negotiations between Henry and Margaret of Austria in 1505. Margaret was the widowed daughter of the Holy Roman Emperor Maximilian I.

Although nothing came of the negotiations, this portrait hung in her palace at Mechelen in Belgium until her death in 1540. Henry appears here as a shrewd and calculating middle-aged man wearing fur-lined robes richly embroidered with gold thread and holding a rose, the all-important symbol of the Tudor dynasty.

Some of the best portraits of monarchs painted from life were produced to exchange with potential marriage partners from foreign courts.

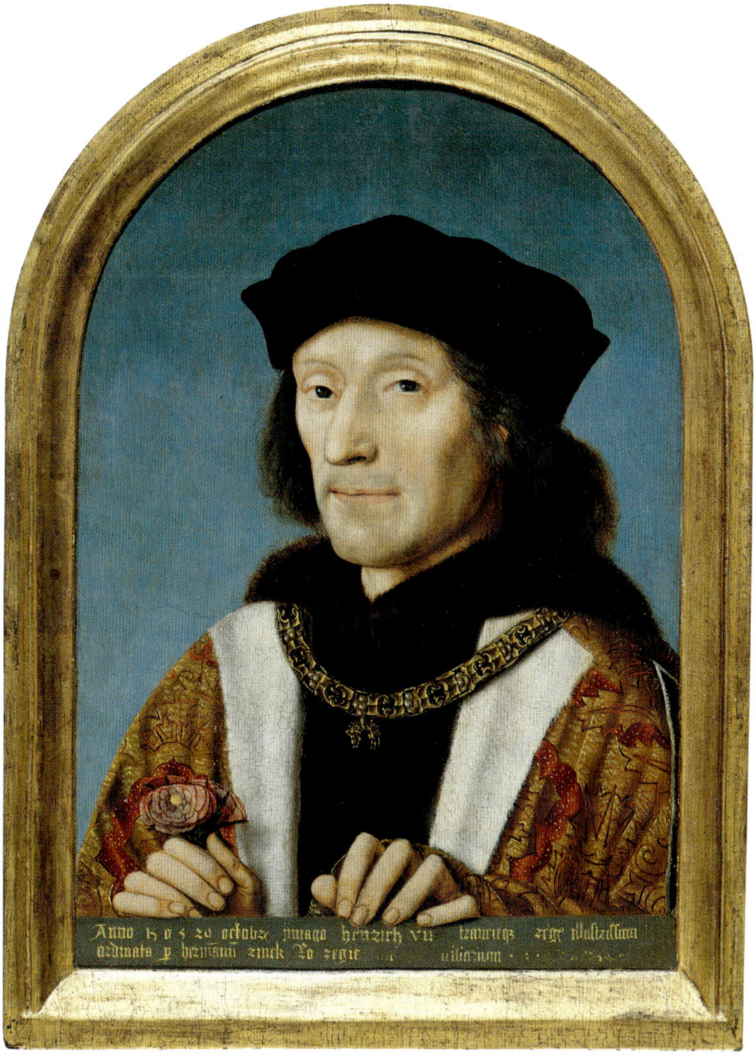

Henry VII
Unknown Netherlandish artist, 1505
Oil on panel, 425 x 305mm
(NPG 416)

Royal family tree 1485–1625

Henry VII reigned 1485–1509 ⁕ Elizabeth of York

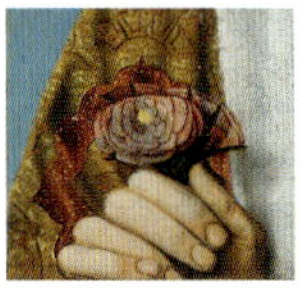

Arthur ⁕ (1) Catherine of Aragon (2) ⁕ (1) **Henry VIII reigned 1509–47**

Margaret ⁕ James IV King of Scots

James V King of Scots

Mary Queen of Scots

James VI of Scotland and **James I of England reigned 1603–25**

Philip II King of Spain ⁕ **Mary I reigned 1553–8**

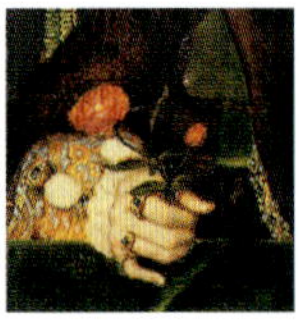

Edward VI reigned 1547–53

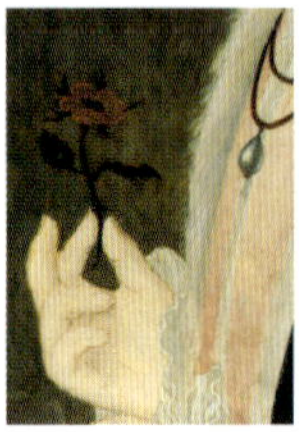

The Tudor rose is seen in many portraits of the royal family and served as a dynastic symbol. The Wars of the Roses (1455–85) came to an end when Henry VII of the House of Lancaster defeated Richard III of the House of York. Henry VII then married Elizabeth of York, and the red rose of Lancaster and the white rose of York were combined into an enduring symbol of Tudor rule.

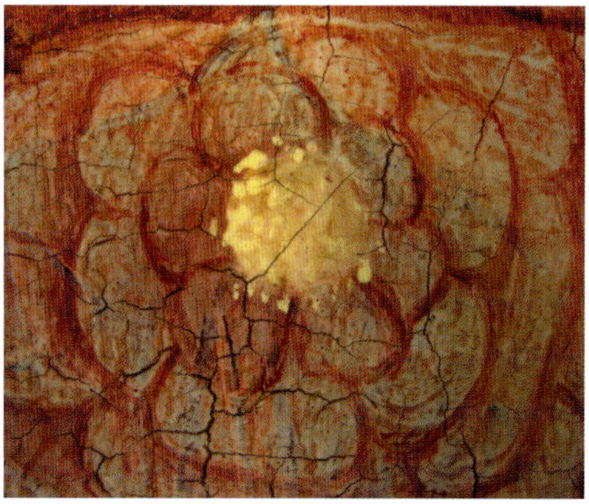

* (2) Anne Boleyn
* (3) Jane Seymour
* (4) Anne of Cleves
* (5) Catherine Howard
* (6) Catherine Parr

Mary * Charles Duke of Suffolk

Frances Brandon * Henry Grey

Elizabeth I
reigned 1558–1603

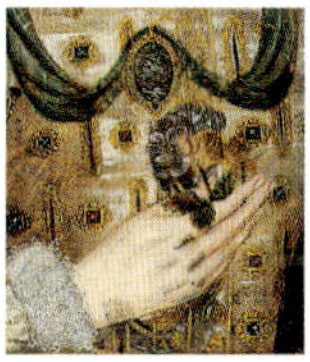

Jane
'Lady Jane Grey'
proclaimed Queen
July 1553

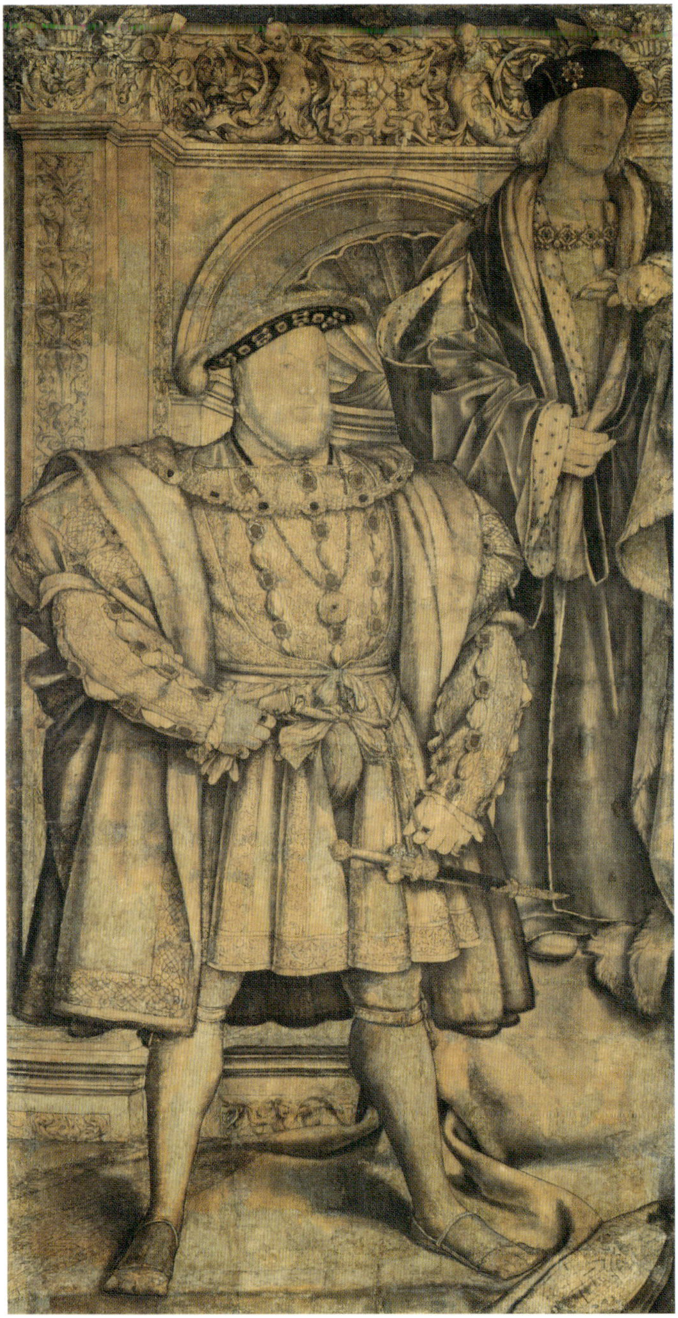

Left: **Henry VIII**
Hans Holbein the Younger (1497/8–1543), *c.*1536–7
Ink and watercolour on paper mounted on canvas, 2578 x 1372mm
(NPG 4027)

Below: **Henry VIII**
Studio of Hans Holbein the Younger, *c.*1545–50
Oil on panel, 2370 x 1205mm
Petworth House
(The National Trust)

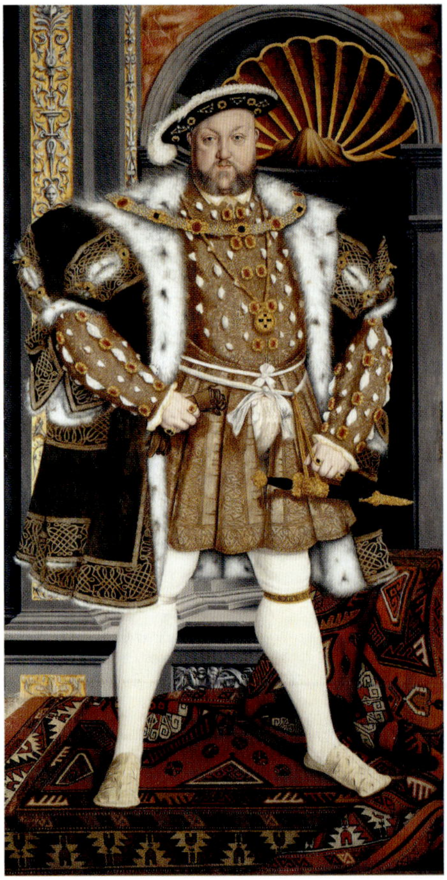

Henry VIII (1491–1547)

Few monarchs have matched Henry VIII's ability to control his public image and impose it on posterity. Undoubtedly the most important portrait of Henry VIII was produced by the émigré artist Hans Holbein the Younger for a large-scale mural painted at Whitehall Palace in 1537. It included his parents and third wife, Jane Seymour. This includes a striking full-length portrait of Henry in a defiant pose with legs astride. Holbein's design only survives in a preparatory drawing, known as a cartoon (opposite far left) as the mural was destroyed in a fire in 1698.

Holbein's likeness of the King was copied and adapted by numerous artists and became the standard face pattern for the remainder of his reign. There are also a number of full-length copies of Henry VIII in existence that were taken from the Whitehall mural. The painting from Petworth House (opposite below left) has the scallop-shell niche behind Henry's head and the carpet that were both found in the original.

The success of Holbein's portrait formula as a tool of propaganda enforcing the King's power and authority is clear when you compare it with other portraits of the King. Another portrait produced by an unknown, but talented, Netherlandish artist shows the King in a more contemplative pose, without any of the characteristics of a determined and authoritative ruler.

Henry VIII
Unknown Netherlandish artist, *c.*1530
Oil on panel,
584 x 445mm
(NPG 3638)

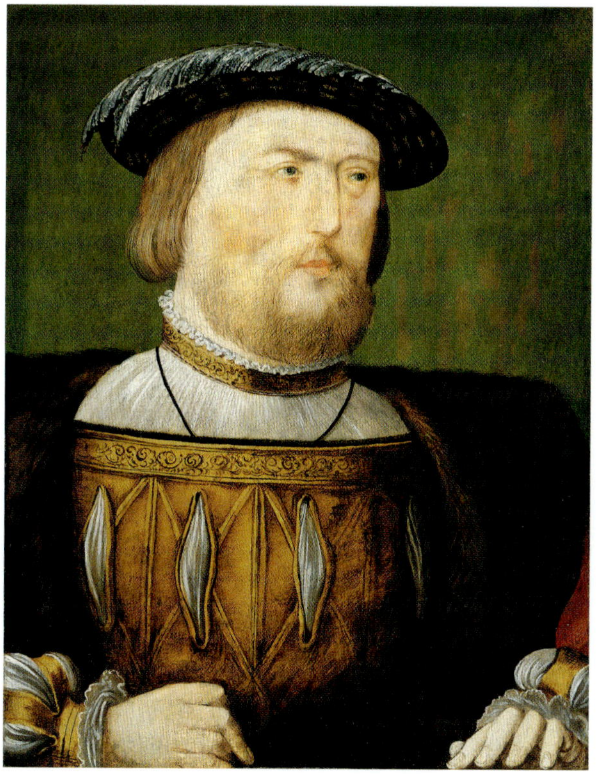

Edward VI (1537–53)
Following the death Henry VIII, his son Edward took up the throne at the age of nine around the time this portrait was painted. He is shown in profile, his delicate youthful features carefully drawn and recorded in paint for posterity. As the much-longed for male heir to the throne, Edward was painted throughout his childhood by several different artists, including the talented German artist Hans Holbein the Younger, indicating his importance and status. This portrait is from the studio of Holbein's successor, another foreign artist called William Scrots. As in all portraits of Edward, the challenge of presenting a young boy as a regal figure and capable potential ruler is partly solved through the adornment of costly clothing and jewellery and the use of an adult-like pose. He died shortly before his sixteenth birthday.

Mary I (1516–58)
Many of the best portraits of the Tudor royal family were painted by German or Netherlandish artists working in England (p.42). Hans Eworth was originally from Antwerp in the Netherlands and worked in London for almost thirty years. Mary I was his most important patron. This portrait shows Mary in her late thirties after her unpopular marriage to Philip II of Spain. Like her grandfather Henry VII (p.27) and her brother Edward VI (below left) she holds a rose, symbolic of the Tudor dynasty.

Mary must have been pleased with this likeness as Eworth produced a number of variants of this portrait, perhaps based on a single sitting from life. Larger than a miniature, but not a life-sized portrait, the picture was designed as a portable object that could be easily held in the hand and stored in a cabinet of precious treasures or sent to foreign courts.

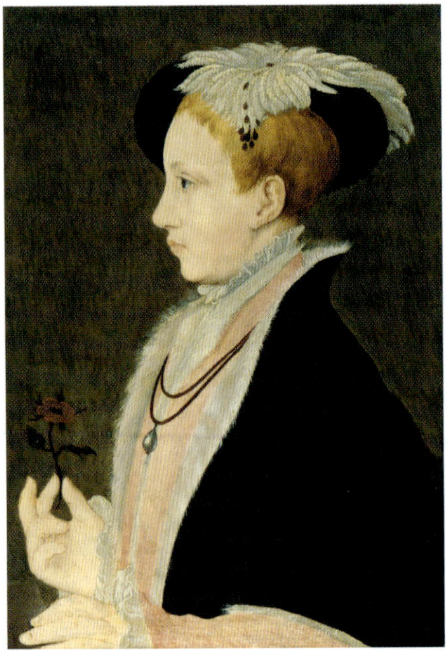

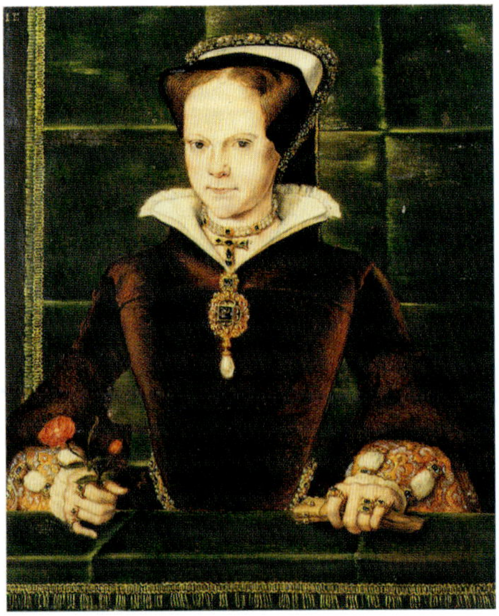

Far left: **Edward VI**
By an artist in the studio of William Scrots (active 1537–53), *c.*1546
Oil on panel, 473 x 279mm
(NPG 442)

Left: **Mary I**
Hans Eworth (active 1540–74), 1554
Oil on panel, 216 x 169mm
(NPG 4861)

Opposite: **'Darnley' portrait of Elizabeth I**
Unknown artist, *c.*1575
Oil on panel, 1130 x 787mm
(NPG 2082)

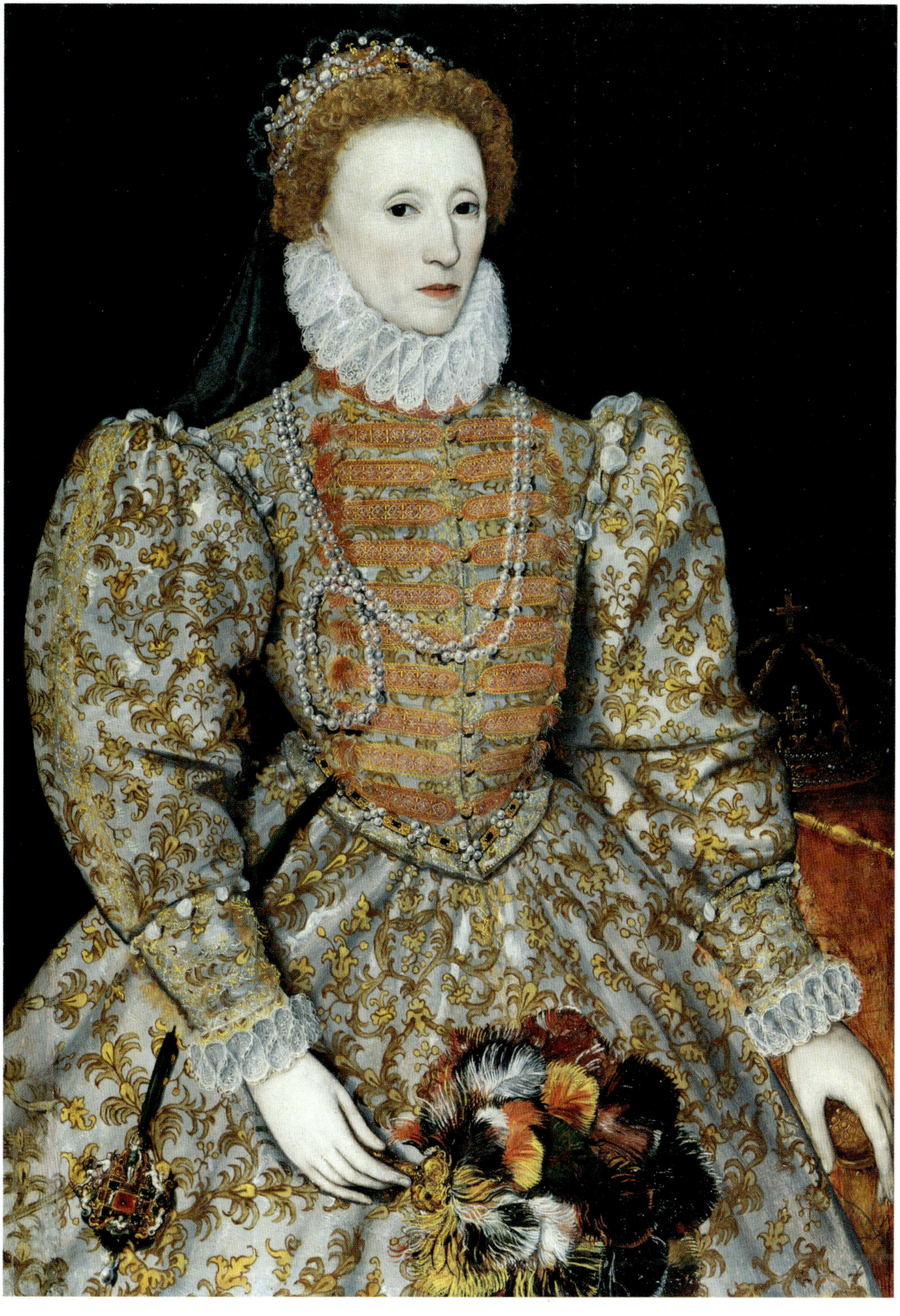

Elizabeth I (1533–1603)

The so-called 'Darnley' portrait of Elizabeth on the previous page, dating from the mid 1570s, is one of the most important portraits of the Queen and was almost certainly painted from life. The facial likeness captured in this portrait was copied for years to come, ensuring that Elizabeth looked many years younger right up to the end of her reign.

Later portraits of Elizabeth I rely increasingly on symbolic attributes championing her virginity. The portrait below, with a maritime scene in the background, celebrates the defeat of the Spanish Armada in 1588. A vast number of pearls – a symbol of purity – adorn the Queen's clothes. In all these portraits, Elizabeth's costume, however elaborate, remains restricted to her personal colours of red, black, gold and white.

It is likely that official royal artist Nicholas Hilliard was called on to create a standardised image of the Queen that would present her as having eternal youth and beauty. In a treatise on miniature painting Hilliard provided an insight into the way the Queen liked to be painted. He records that she disliked shadows and chose to be painted in the 'alley of a goodly garden', which gave bright and even lighting across her features.

A remarkable full-length portrait at Hardwick Hall in Derbyshire shows the Queen aged about sixty-six, in the last years of her reign (below and inside front cover). Elizabeth I displays no signs of age or infirmity. The legendary noblewoman Bess of Hardwick commissioned the portrait. Elizabeth's impressive skirt is richly embroidered with dragons, sea serpents, fish, flowers and birds.

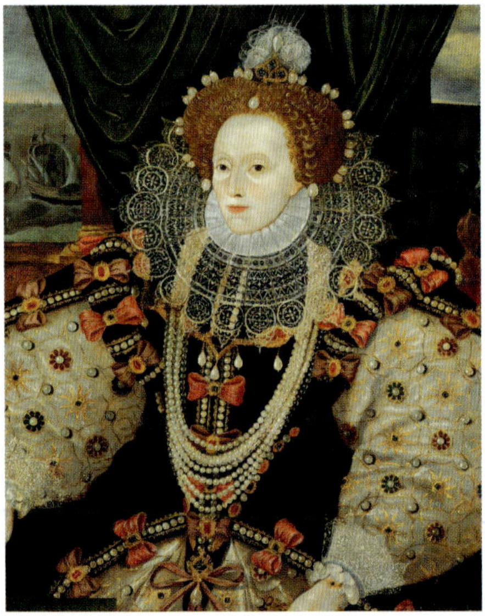

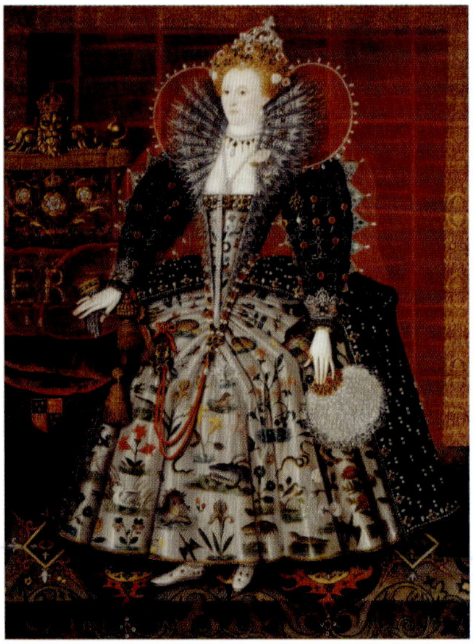

Far left: **'Armada' portrait of Elizabeth I**
Attributed to George Gower (*c*.1540–96), *c*.1588
Oil on panel,
978 x 724mm
(NPG 541)

Left: **Elizabeth I**
Studio of Nicholas Hilliard, *c*.1599
Oil on panel,
2230 x 1650mm
Hardwick Hall
(The National Trust)

James I (1566–1625)

As with portraits of Elizabeth I, most of the portraits of her successor James I were not painted from life but were based on a pattern taken from one of the few sittings the King had with favoured artists. This portrait is a version of a popular portrait type of James and shows him soon after his accession to the throne of England and Wales. It was painted after a design by the King's 'Serjeant' or official painter who was responsible for producing both decorative works and portraits for the king. James is shown wearing an elaborate hat jewel, set with huge diamonds, known as the 'feather'.

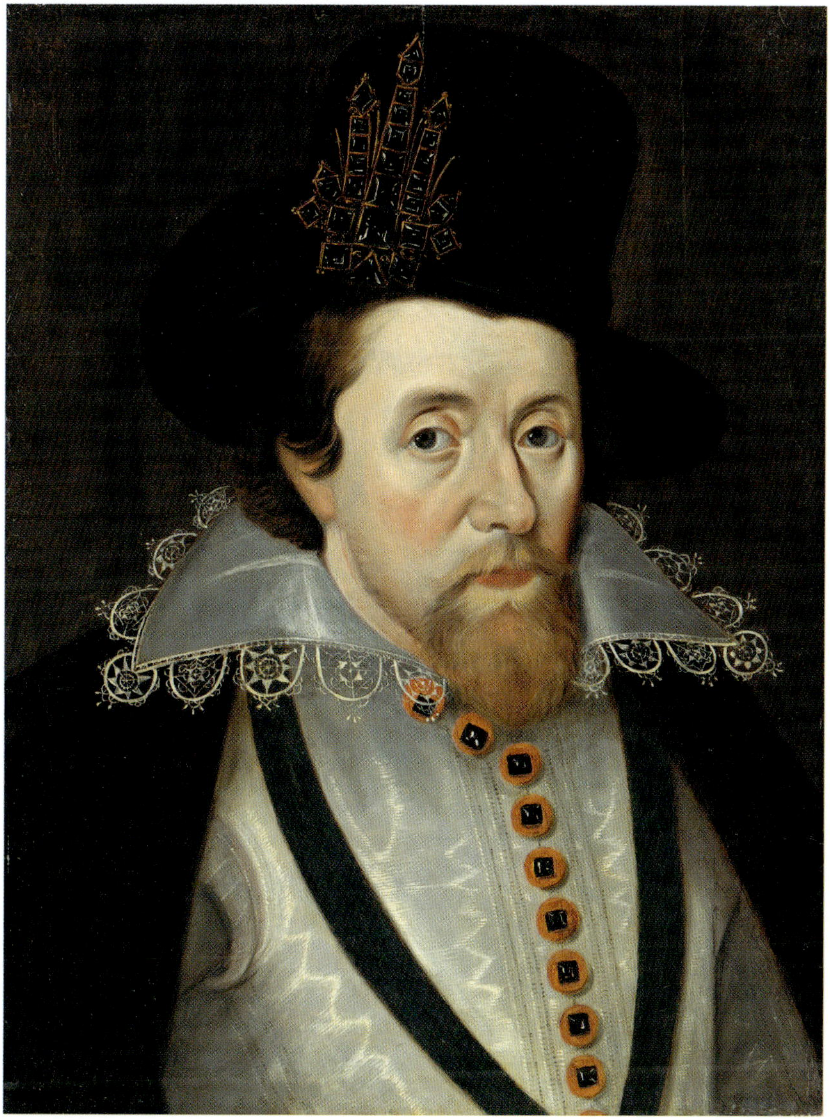

James I (1566–1625)
Unknown artist after
John De Critz the Elder
(*c.*1551/2–1642), *c.*1606
Oil on panel,
572 x 419mm
(NPG 548)

Family portraits

Like family photographs today, painted portraits of individual family members were a regular feature of the Tudor domestic interior for wealthy home-owners. In contrast to the Netherlands where group portraiture was popular, large-scale group portraits were not common in Tudor England. Group family portraits were, however, sometimes painted to celebrate the revival of family fortunes or at moments of family crisis following the death of the heir. In these instances portraiture helped establish a new family hierarchy or provided a link between past and future, as with the portrait of the family of Sir Thomas More (pp.38–9) and the double portrait of Mary Neville, Lady Dacre and her son (right).

Large-scale group portraits became easier to produce with the introduction of canvas stretched over a frame. Canvas began to replace wooden panels as the artist's choice of support for all types of painting in the 1590s and the first few decades of the seventeenth century.

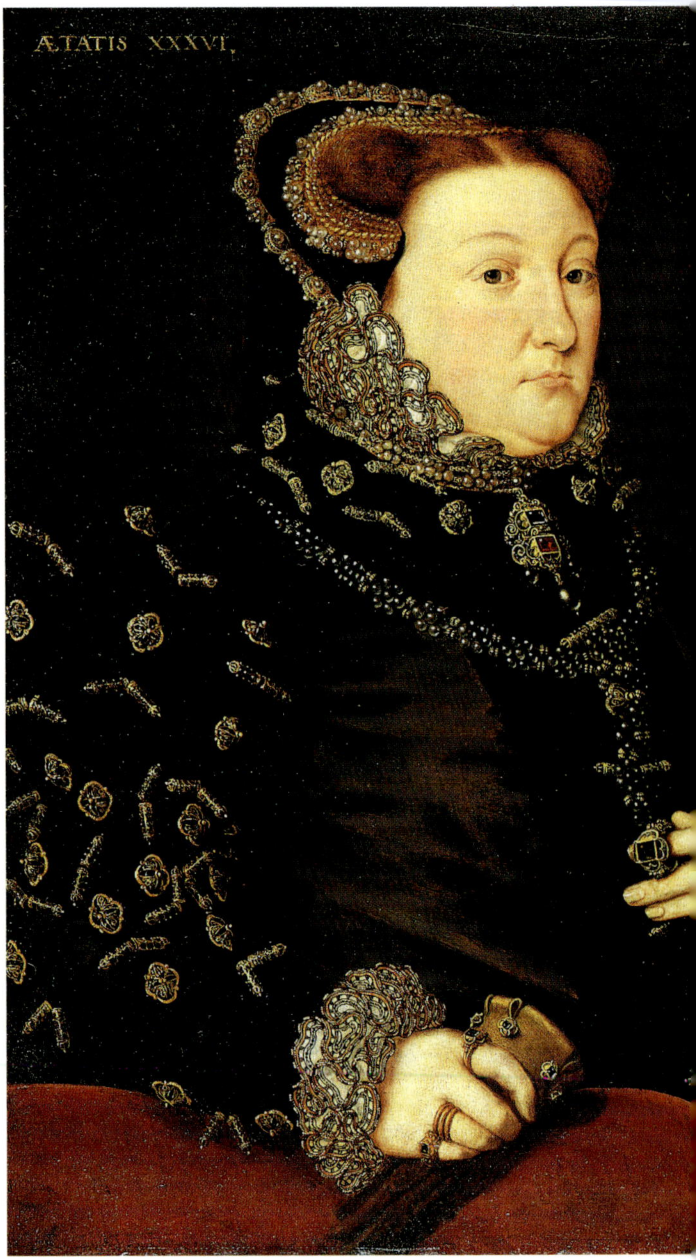

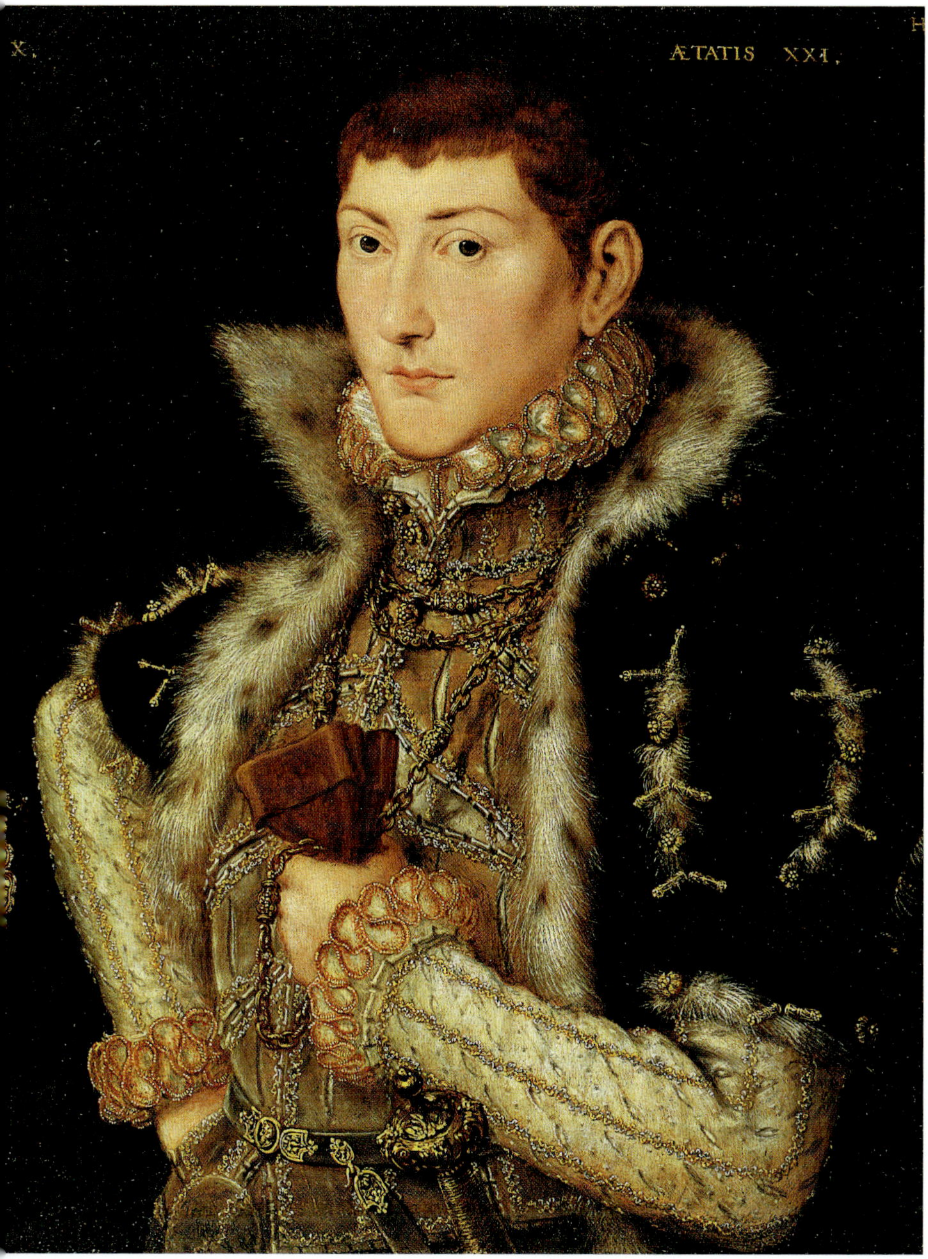

Mary Neville, Lady Dacre and her son Gregory Fiennes, 10th Baron Dacre
Hans Eworth (active 1540–74), 1559
Oil on panel,
500 x 714mm
(NPG L185)

Mary Neville, Lady Dacre (died c.1576) and her son Gregory Fiennes, 10th Baron Dacre (1539–94)
The portrait of a mother and son on the previous page is very unusual since double portraits usually showed husbands and wives. Gregory's father was executed for his involvement in a hunting incident in which a gamekeeper had been killed and as a consequence the family was stripped of its title. This portrait celebrates the restoration of family honour and the official title of Baron to Gregory Fiennes in 1559.

Sir Thomas More (1478–1535), his father, his household and descendants
This portrait shows five generations of the family of the scholar and Lord Chancellor of England Sir Thomas More. It presents a fiction by showing living and dead family members together in the same room. More's grandson commissioned it long after the Lord Chancellor's death, and it is partly based on an earlier group portrait by Hans Holbein showing More's immediate family, which is now lost.

More was executed by Henry VIII in 1535 for refusing to accept the king as the Head of the Church of England and became a Roman Catholic martyr. He is seated third from the left wearing a gold chain and a dark red cloak. The four figures to the right wearing Elizabethan ruffs represent the later generations and, like their ancestors, they hold prayer books signalling their piety. Part of the painting's purpose was to show that faith could not be disrupted by the death of a family member or changed political circumstances.

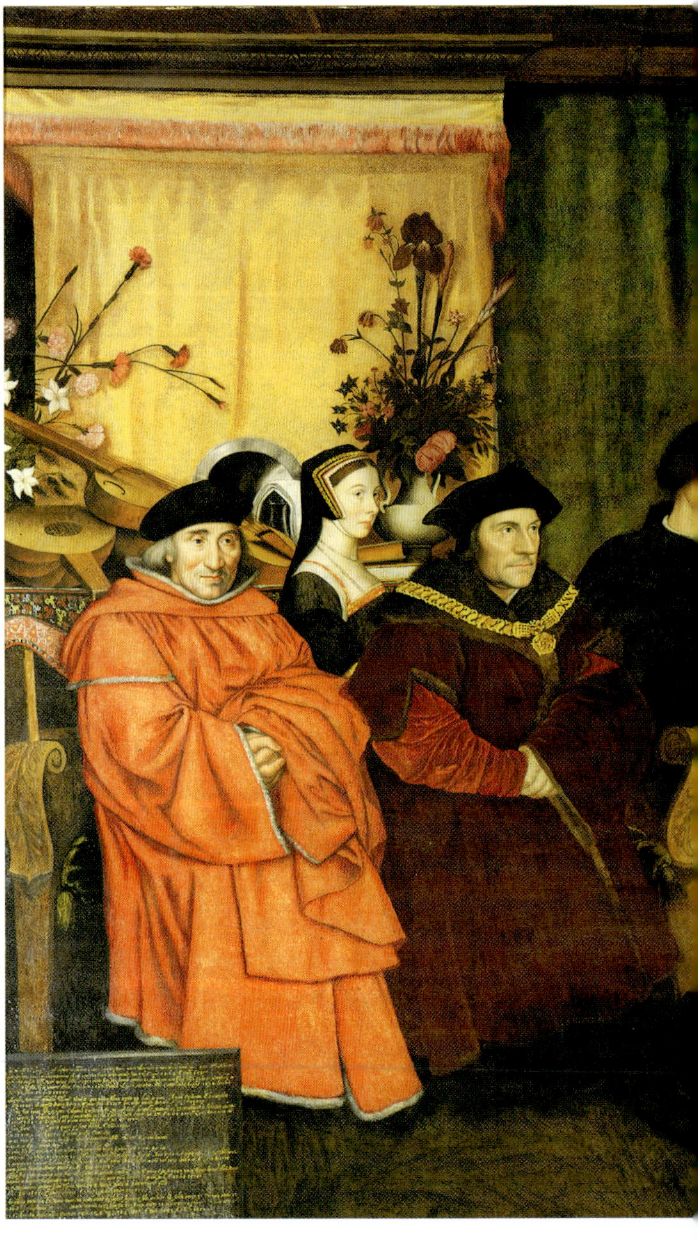

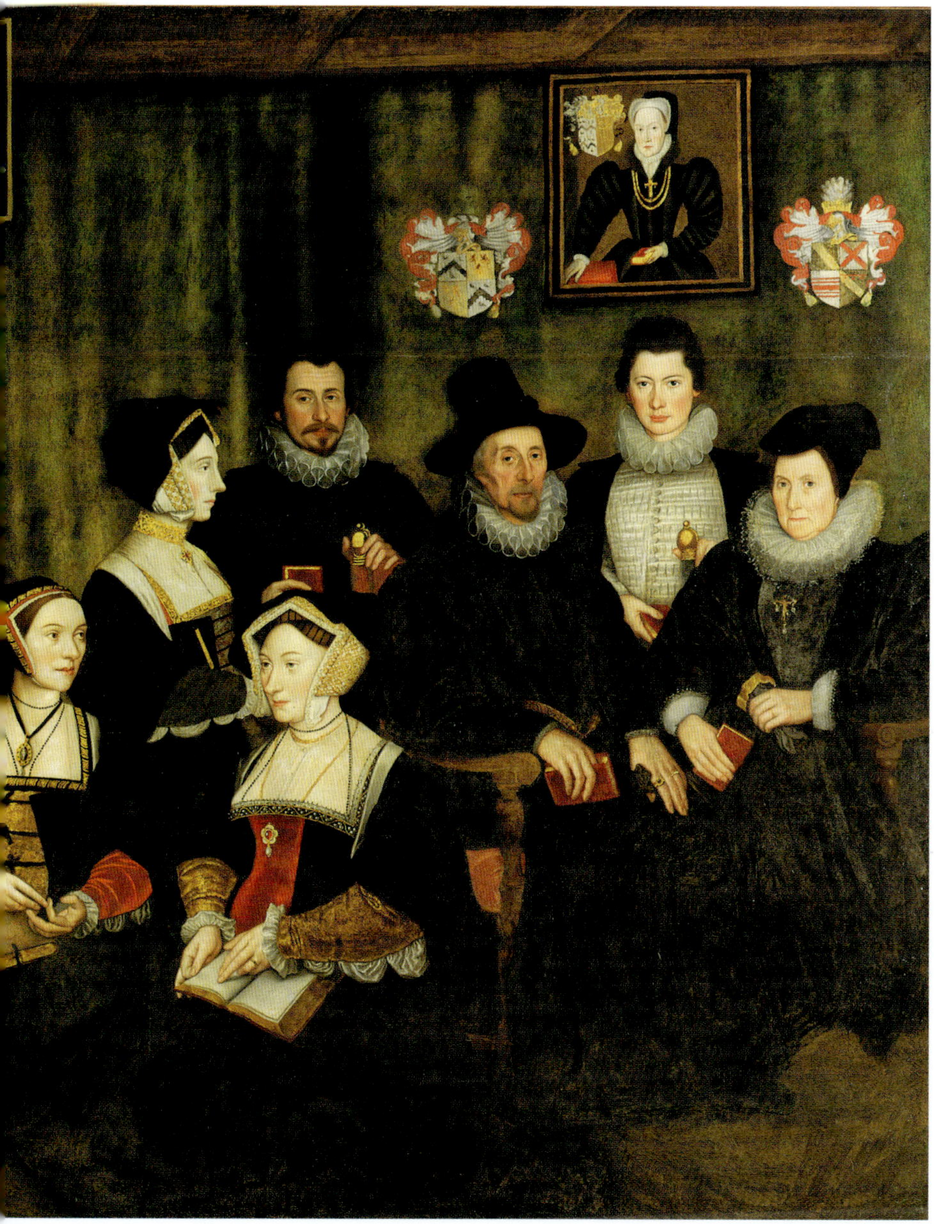

Sir Thomas More, his father, his household and descendants
Rowland Lockey
(*c.*1566–1616), 1593
Oil on canvas,
2274 x 3302mm
(NPG 2765)

The Carey family
Attributed to Paul Van Somer (1577/8–1621/2), *c.*1617
Oil on canvas, 2273 x 2165mm
(NPG 5246)

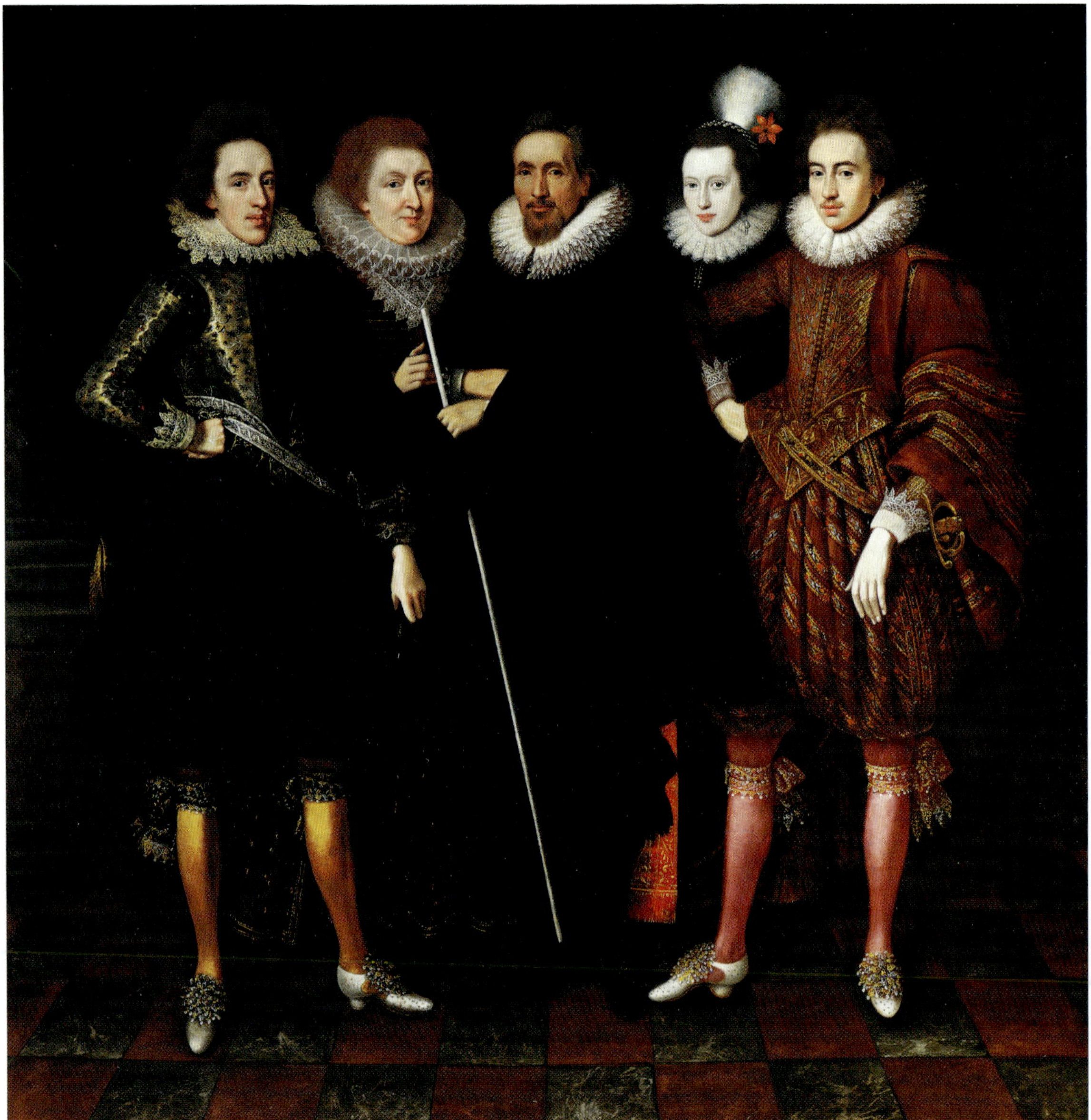

Robert Carey (later 1st Earl of Monmouth, 1560?–1639), his wife Elizabeth Trevannion (d.1641), and their children Henry (1596–1661), Philadelphia (1594–1654) and Thomas (1597–1634)
This life-sized portrait depicts the family of Robert Carey, a soldier and courtier at the court of James I. It was painted in 1617 when Robert Carey was made Chamberlain to Prince Charles, and Robert is seen at the centre of this proud family group holding a long white rod of office. The two young sons (aged around twenty and twenty-one) show off their glamorous finery at either side of their parents, while their older sister peers out over their shoulders, standing to the back.

Children of Sir Thomas Lucy III (1585–1640)
This group portrait depicts four children of Sir Thomas Lucy, a successful courtier and magistrate who lived at Charlecote Park in Warwickshire. From left to right, the children are: Bridget (aged two), Richard (one), Constance (five) and Margaret (three). Richard Lucy, sitting in the chair, inherited Charlecote in 1658.

A large-scale painting with numerous figures would have taken considerable planning, and the faces would probably have been painted from individual studies. The clothing may have been arranged on a dummy or another stand-in figure, which meant the children would not have had to pose for any length of time.

Four of Sir Thomas Lucy III's children
Cornelius Johnson (1593–1661), 1619
Oil on panel, 1245 x 1700mm
Charlecote Park (The National Trust)

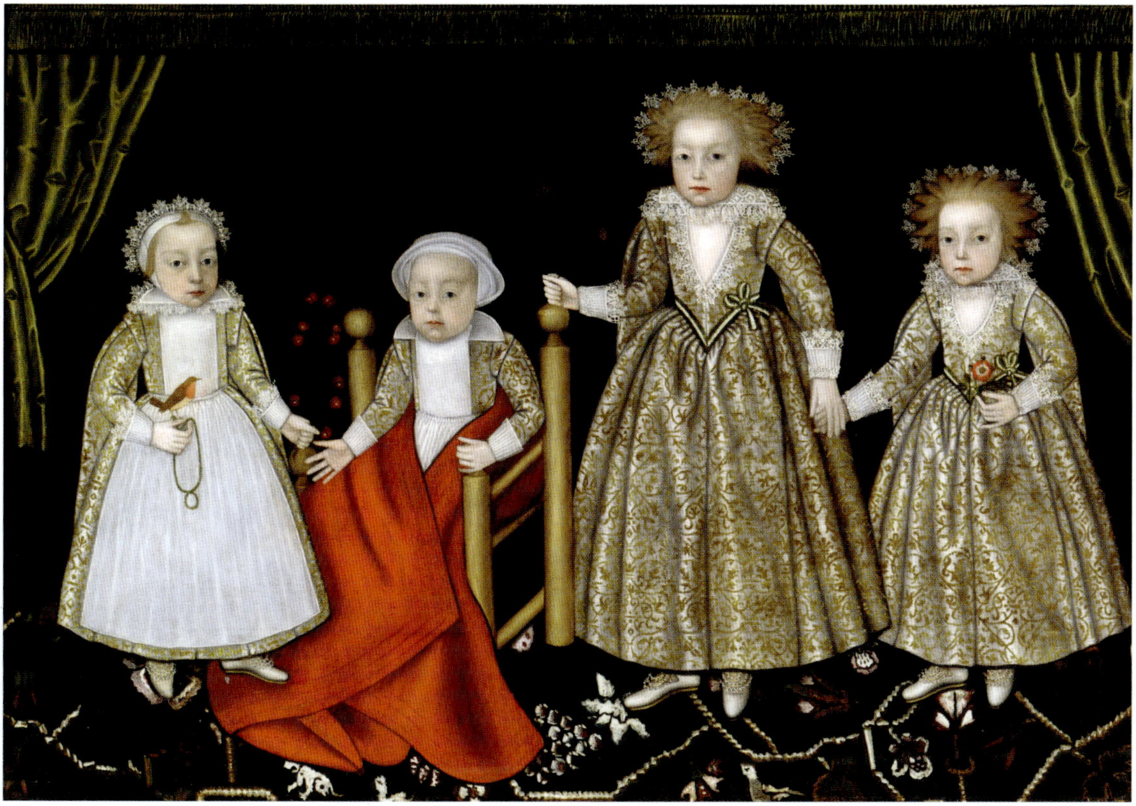

Artists and how they worked

Unfortunately we know very little about many of the artists who painted portraits in this period. Few painters signed their pictures and while we can sometimes link groups of pictures to a particular workshop, pinpointing the identity of an individual artist is more difficult.

Artists as craftsmen

Most painters shared the same status as other artisans and craftsmen, although they would not have claimed the prestige or salary of an expert goldsmith or tapestry weaver. Painters could produce portraits to an established formula, as well as taking on other types of work, such as painting signs, banners and other decorative items.

Distinguished artists

Artists who managed to distinguish themselves did so through working for the crown or high-ranking courtiers. Most artists who held official positions at court were immigrants, mainly from northern Europe. Their style and techniques were very influential in England. The German artist Gerlach Flicke (active c.1495–1558), the Dutch man Marcus Gheeraerts the Younger (1561/2–1636) and the Flemish artist Michiel Jansz. van Miereveldt (1567–1641) are examples of painters who forged successful careers in England. However, some English artists did achieve prominence as painters of life-sized portraits, in particular George Gower (c.1540–96), who served as an official painter to Queen Elizabeth. He painted the portraits of Elizabeth I (p.34, left) and Elizabeth Knollys (p.17).

Acclaimed artists who worked directly for the monarch might earn considerable sums: Hans Holbein the Younger (1497/8–1543) was paid £30 per year but also received extra payments for individual pictures and, in the early Elizabethan period, the Flemish female artist Levina Teerlinc (c.1510–76) received £40 per year (the cost of a moderately sized house).

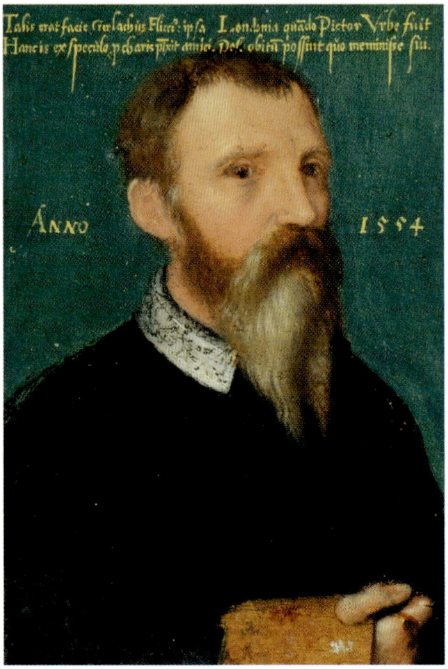

Self-portrait of Gerlach Flicke, 1554
Left-hand panel of a diptych, oil on paper or vellum laid on panel, 88 x 119mm (NPG 6353)

Analysing portraits

Some of the questions about how artists worked are answered by studying early artists' treatises. Technology also allows us to look beneath the paint's surface to reveal the various stages of the composition. Techniques, such as X-ray, infrared photography and the sampling of microscopic fragments of paint, provide some fascinating information about the materials and techniques in use during this period. Technology can also be used to find out approximately when a portrait was painted.

Making portraits

The production of portraits involved a painter, a sitter and sometimes a third party such as the patron; all these people had a say on how the finished portrait looked. Infrared photography reveals that the German artist Gerlach Flicke had noted down the colours of one individual element of his portrait of Thomas Cranmer on his preliminary drawing as an instruction or as a memory aid. Beneath the crimson coloured cushion on the right, the word 'rot' (the German word for red) can be seen (below centre right). This type of notation allowed artists to remember the exact specifications of a patron or the correct colours of fabrics.

Right: **Thomas Cranmer**
Gerlach Flicke, 1545
Oil on panel,
984 x 762mm
(NPG 535)

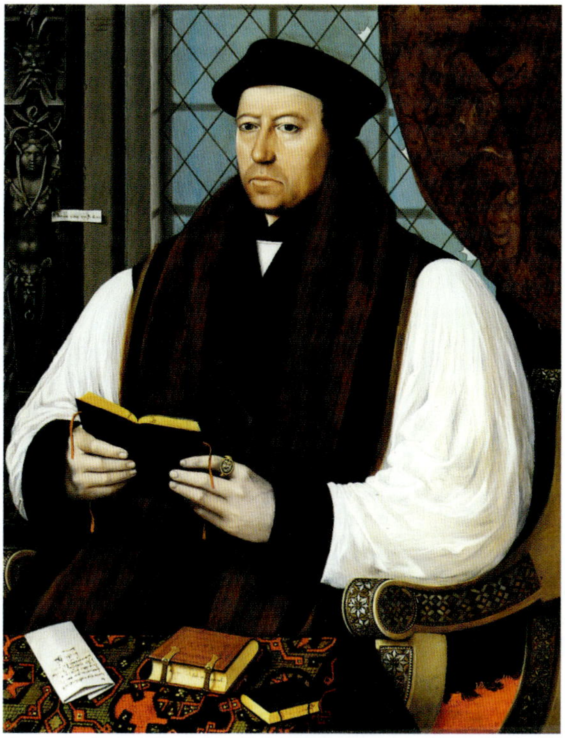

Far right: details from the portrait of **Thomas Cranmer**

Above: the left eye under magnification shows Flicke's painting technique and accomplished style.

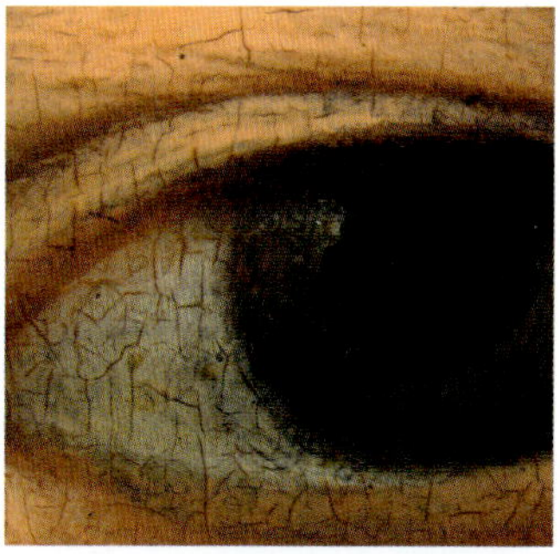

Centre: this detail of an infrared photograph shows the word 'rot' (red) beneath the arm of the chair.

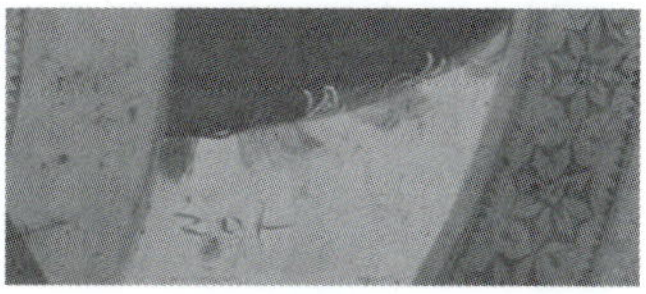

Below: detail of the red cushion

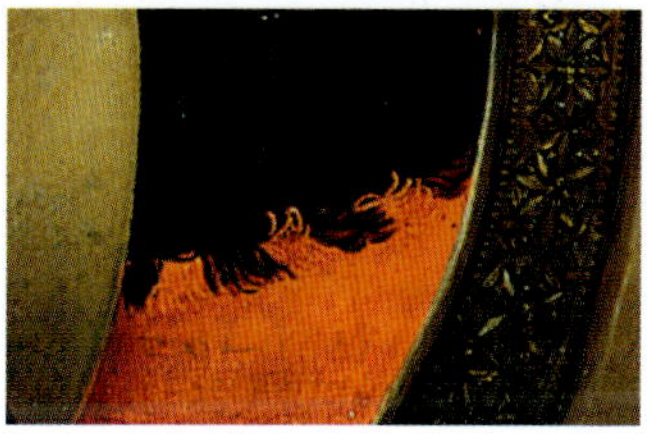

Panels and canvases

Artists typically painted on oak boards joined together and chiselled down to produce a reasonably thin panel with a flat surface. The thin wooden panels were expensive and time-consuming to make. In England artists used oak, usually imported from the Baltic region. From the late 1590s canvas was increasingly used as a support since it was better suited to large-scale paintings.

Reusing panels

When portraits were abandoned or not paid for, there was clearly no sense in letting a good piece of wood go to waste, and occasionally artists reused old panels. A newly commissioned portrait might have been painted over the original work without the new owner knowing what once lay beneath.

This occurred in the case of a portrait of Elizabeth I dated about 1580 (below); it was painted on top of an apparently unfinished portrait of an unknown lady who wears a costume dating from a decade or so earlier. As portraits of Elizabeth I were popular items that could be sold from stock, the artist was reasonably sure of a sale in this instance.

Below left: **Elizabeth I**
Unknown artist, *c.*1575–80
Oil on panel,
666 x 488mm
(NPG 200)

Below: **X-ray of Elizabeth I**
The unknown lady is facing in the opposite direction, her eyes can be seen on the forehead to the left of the Queen's eyes.

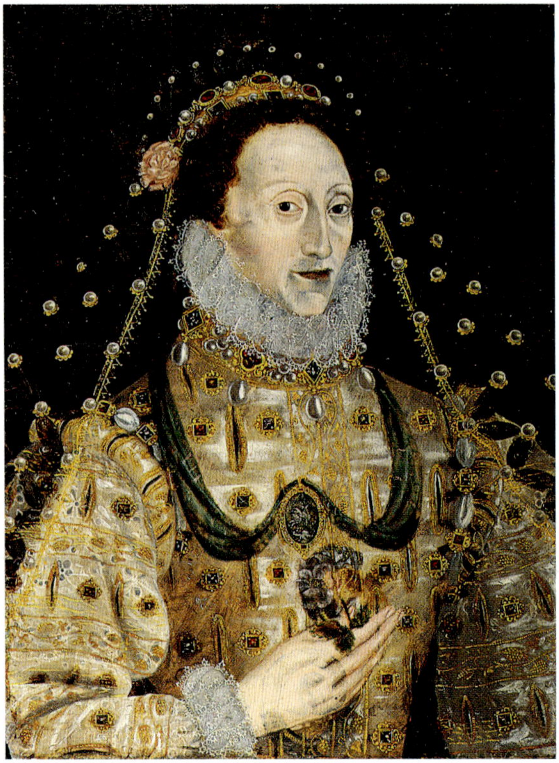

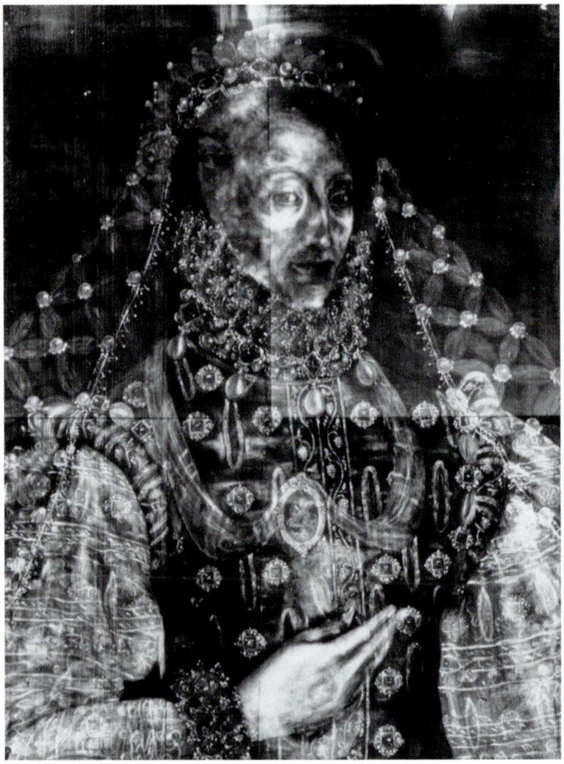

Artists' techniques

Artists or their apprentices would seal the wooden panels or canvas with an animal glue, known as size. They would prepare an even white ground surface by applying a mixture of chalk bound with size.

The designs for compositions were transferred onto the primed wooden panel or canvas by various means. The preparatory drawing could be drawn freehand, but an artist needing to transfer a finished drawing as accurately as possible might use a cartoon. Lines drawn on paper would be pricked and then pounced, which involved dusting charcoal or carbon powder through the holes. The dots of charcoal, left on the panel or canvas when the cartoon was removed, were then joined to complete the composition. This method was used in the portrait of Mary I by Master John (below).

The layers of oil paint would be built up covering the under drawing. Finally, the painting was finished with a varnish to protect the surface and bring out the full brilliancy of the colours.

It was common for artists to make numerous adjustments to the composition during both the drawing and painting processes. For example, the artist might choose to reposition the hands or to adjust the proportions of the body. Occasionally, new features, such as coats of arms or items of jewellery, were added, probably at the request of the patron.

Pigments, varnishes and brushes

Raw materials, such as pigments and varnishes, could be purchased from grocers and apothecaries and were mainly imported from overseas. An apprentice usually mixed the paints, which were then stored in pouches made from a pig's bladder. Paint brushes, called 'pencils', were made from the hair of squirrels' tails, from sable (an animal like a stoat) or from hogs' hair. Squirrel and sable brushes were used for very fine work.

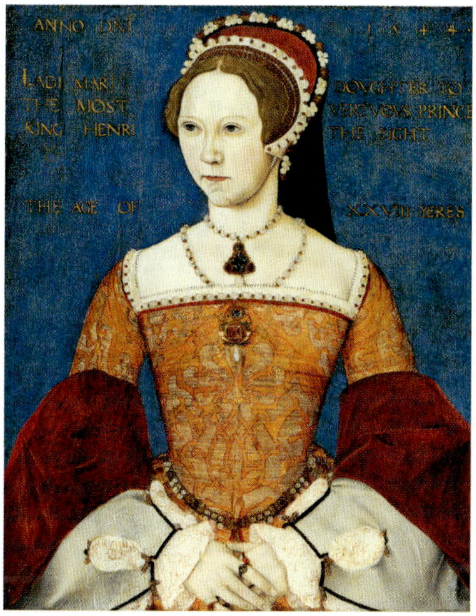

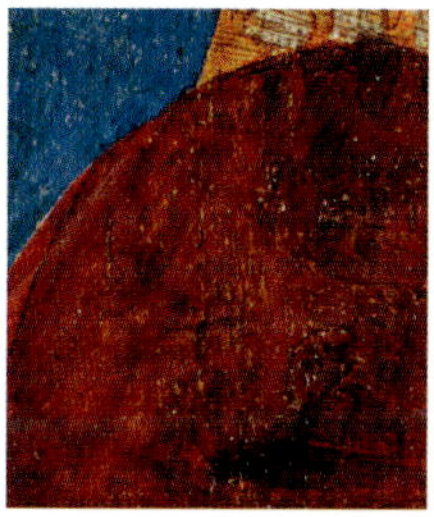

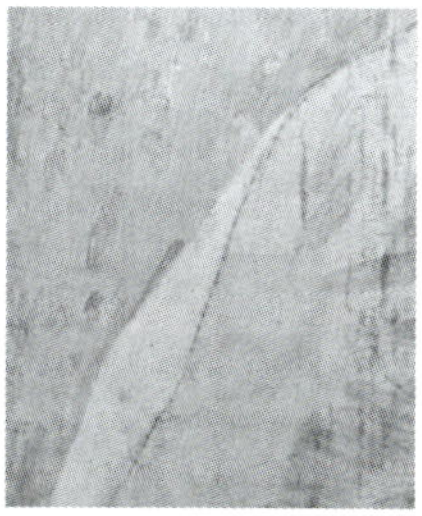

Right: **Mary I**
Master John (active 1544–*c*.50), 1544
Oil on panel,
711 x 508mm
(NPG 428)

Centre right: detail of Mary I's sleeve that corresponds with the area shown in the infrared photograph to the right.

Far right: this infrared photograph shows evidence of the use of a cartoon. The dots of charcoal on the under drawing have been joined together to create the shape of her sleeve.

Collections to visit

You can see more Tudor and Jacobean portraits at the National Portrait Gallery, St Martin's Place, London WC2H 0HE or visit our website: www.npg.org.uk

Many of the National Portrait Gallery's most important portraits of the period can also be seen on display in the long gallery at Montacute House, Montacute, Somerset, TA15 6XP.

Here is a selection of other National Trust properties in Britain where you can see Tudor and Jacobean portraits:

South of England
Claydon House
Middle Claydon
Near Buckingham
Buckinghamshire
MK18 2EY

Ham House
Ham Street
Ham
Richmond-upon-Thames
TW10 7RS

The Vyne
Sherborne St John
Basingstoke
Hampshire RG24 9HL

East of England
Anglesey Abbey
Quy Road
Lode
Cambridge
Cambridgeshire
CB25 9EJ

Blickling Hall
Blickling
Norwich
Norfolk NR11 6NF

Oxburgh Hall
Oxburgh
King's Lynn
Norfolk PE33 9PS

South East
Knole
Sevenoaks
Kent TN15 0RP

Petworth House
Petworth
West Sussex GU28 0AE

East Midlands
Hardwick Hall
Doe Lea
Chesterfield
Derbyshire S44 5QJ

West Midlands
Charlecote Park
Warwick
Warwickshire
CV35 9ER

Coughton Court
Near Alcester
Warwickshire
B49 5JA

Wessex
Dunster Castle
Dunster
Near Minehead
Somerset TA24 6SL

Kingston Lacy
Wimborne Minster
Dorset BH21 4EA

Lacock Abbey
Lacock
Near Chippenham
Wiltshire SN5 2LG

Lytes Cary Manor
Near Charlton Mackrell
Somerton
Somerset TA11 7HU

Devon and Cornwall
Antony
Torpoint
Cornwall PL11 2QA

Buckland Abbey
Yelverton
Devon PL20 6EY

Compton Castle
Marldon
Paignton
Devon TQ3 1TA

Cotehele
St Dominick
Near Saltash
Cornwall PL12 6tA

Wales
Plas Newydd
Llanfairpwll
Anglesey LL61 6DQ

Powis Castle
Welshpool
Powys
Wales SY21 8RF

For further information, opening times and admission prices, visit the National Trust website at www.nationaltrust.org.uk

Some other properties in Britain open to the public where you can see Tudor and Jacobean portraits include:

Burghley House, Lincolnshire;
Gwydir Castle, North Wales;
Hatfield House, Hertfordshire;
Hever Castle, Kent;
Kirby Hall, Northamptonshire;
Kenwood House, London;
Longleat, Wiltshire;
Rockingham Castle, Leicestershire;
and Sudeley Castle, Gloucestershire.

Further sources for studying the period

J. Ashelford,
Dress in the Age of Elizabeth I,
Batsford, London, 1988

BBC history website:
www.bbc.co.uk/history/british/tudors/

E. Chaney and P. Mack,
England and the Continental Renaissance,
Boydell, Woodbridge, 1990

K. Coombs,
The Portrait Miniature in England,
V&A Publications, London, 1998

K. Hearn,
Dynasties: Painting in Tudor and Jacobean England 1530–1630,
Tate Gallery Publications, London, 1995

M. Howard,
The Tudor Image,
Tate Gallery Publications, London, 1995

R. Strong,
Gloriana: The Portraits of Elizabeth I,
Pimlico, London, 2003

Acknowledgements and picture credits

Author's acknowledgements
I am extremely grateful to Catharine MacLeod whose previous publications, *Tudor and Jacobean Portraits in the National Portrait Gallery Collection at Montacute House* (1999) and *Tudor Portraits* (2000), provided a starting point for this book. I am also indebted to my hardworking curatorial interns Nicola Pickering and Natasha Broad, and to Sophie Plender who provided invaluable information on artists and how they worked. I would also like to thank Alastair Laing, Curator of Pictures and Sculpture at the National Trust, and his assistant Alison Fuller for their advice and valuable information. I am very grateful to Antonia Fraser for writing the foreword with such enthusiasm. Finally I would like to thank the editor Caroline Brooke Johnson and the designers Thomas Manss and Vita Piccolomini for their enthusiasm and hard work in making this book happen.

Picture credits
The publisher would like to thank the copyright holders for granting permission to reproduce works illustrated in this book. Every effort has been made to contact the holders of copyright material, and any omissions will be corrected in future editions if the publisher is notified in writing.

All pictures are the copyright of the National Portrait Gallery unless otherwise stated: p.11 **Long Gallery**, Montacute House (The National Trust), ©NTPL; p.17 **Elizabeth Knollys, Lady Layton**, Montacute House, Sir Malcolm Stewart Bequest (The National Trust), ©NTPL/Derrick E. Witty; p.23 **Sir John Luttrell**, Dunster Castle, The Luttrell Collection (The National Trust), ©NTPL/ John Hammond; p.30 **Henry VIII**, Petworth House, The Egremont Collection (acquired *in lieu* of tax by H.M. Treasury in 1957 and subsequently transferred to the National Trust), ©NTPL/Derrick E. Witty; p.34 **Queen Elizabeth I**, Hardwick Hall, The Devonshire Collection (acquired through the National Land Fund and transferred to The National Trust in 1959), ©NTPL/John Hammond; p.41 **Four children of Sir Thomas Lucy III**, Charlecote Park, The Fairfax-Lucy Collection (The National Trust), ©NTPL/ Derrick E Witty.

Front cover:
Detail from **Mary Throckmorton, Lady Scudamore** (p.18)

Back cover:
Mary Throckmorton, Lady Scudamore (p.18)

Inside front cover:
Detail from **Elizabeth I** (p.34, right)

Inside back cover:
Henry, Prince of Wales
Marcus Gheeraerts the Younger, *c.*1603
Oil on canvas, 1619 x 1168mm
(NPG 2562)

Published in Great Britain by
National Portrait Gallery Publications
National Portrait Gallery
St Martin's Place
London WC2H 0HE

In association with
The National Trust
Heelis
Kemble Drive
Swindon
Wiltshire SN2 2NA

For a complete catalogue of current publications please write to the address above, or visit our website at www.npg.org.uk

ISBN 978 1 185514 393 7

A catalogue record for this book is available from the British Library.

Publishing Manager: Celia Joicey
Editor: Caroline Brooke Johnson
Design: Thomas Manss & Company
Production Manager: Ruth Müller-Wirth
Microscopic photography: Sally Marriott
Printed and bound in Hong Kong

10 9 8 7 6 5 4 3 2